COLL

Cycling *in* NORTHUMBERLAND & NORTH EAST ENGLAND

TED SMART

This edition produced for The Book People Ltd
Hall Wood Avenue, Haydock,
St Helens WA11 9UL

Published by Collins
An imprint of HarperCollins*Publishers*
77-85 Fulham Palace Road
London W6 8JB

First published 2000

Routes compiled by Paul Fox, Pauline Fox and Dave Coltman.
Design by Creative Matters Design Consultancy, Glasgow.
Typeset by Bob Vickers.

Photographs reproduced by kind permission of the following:
Bill Meadows Picture Library pages 11, 39, 57; Britain on View/Stockwave
pages 5, 17, 26, 30, 33, 36, 41, 48, 53, 61, 65, 73, 77, 91, 99, 107;
Northumbria Tourist Board pages 8 (Graeme Peacock), 20 (Gateshead MBC), 104.

Printed in Singapore

ISBN 0 00 760497 1
23/02/00

CONTENTS

KEY TO ROUTES

Route		Grade	Distance km (miles)	Time to allow	Page
1	Boulmer and Alnmouth	moderate	16 (10)	2 hours	14
2	The Tyne Valley – Newburn to Ovingham	easy	19 (12)	3 hours	16
3	The Angel of the North and Beamish	strenuous	20 (12.5)	3–5 hours	19
4	Derwent Valley Railway Path – Newcastle to Rowlands Gill	easy	22.5 (14)	2–4 hours	22
5	Ford and Etal	moderate	24 (15)	2–3 hours	25
6	Corbridge, Hadrian's Wall and Aydon Castle	moderate	24 (15)	3–4 hours	28
7	Craster and Dunstanburgh Castle	easy	31.5 (19.5)	3–4 hours	31
8	Mitford and Bolam	easy	33.5 (21)	3–5 hours	34
9	Hexham, Blanchland and Corbridge	strenuous	40 (25)	5–6 hours	37
10	Durham, Binchester and Bishop Auckland	easy	48 (30)	3–4 hours	41
11	Durham Dales – Stanhope to Middleton Teesdale	strenuous	49.5 (31)	4–5 hours	45
12	Hamsterley, Barnard Castle and Staindrop	moderate	51.5 (32)	4–6 hours	49
13	Felton, Druridge Bay and Morpeth	easy	54.5 (34)	3–4 hours	52
14	Chatton and Holy Island	moderate	59.5 (37)	4–6 hours	56
15	Derwent Valley Railway Path – Rowlands Gill to Waskerley	moderate	59.5 (37)	5–7 hours	60
16	The Tees Valley – Sedgefield to Yarm	easy	62.5 (39)	4–5 hours	64
17	Bellingham and Kielder Reservoir	strenuous	62.5 (39)	5 hours	68
18	Allendale, Allenheads and Blanchland	strenuous	63.5 (39.5)	6–8 hours	72
19	Belsay, Chesters Roman Fort and Hexham	strenuous	73 (45.5)	5–7 hours	76
20	Wooler, Kirk Yetholm and Branxton	moderate	74 (46)	5–7 hours	81
21	Cambo, Rothbury and Elsdon	strenuous	74 (46)	10 hours	85
22	Hadrian's Wall – Vindolanda, Housesteads and Birdoswald	strenuous	75.5 (47)	6–8 hours	90
23	Bamburgh, Alnwick and Ros Castle	moderate	80.5 (50)	5–8 hours	95
24	Ponteland, Simonburn and Wark	strenuous	96.5 (60)	7–9 hours	101
25	Northumberland – a grande randonnée	moderate	142.5 (89)	1–2 days	106

Distances have been rounded up or down to the nearest 0.5km (mile).

Route colour coding

undemanding rides compiled specifically with families in mind
15–25km (10–15 miles)

middle distance rides suitable for all cyclists
25–40km (15–25 miles)

half-day rides for the more experienced and adventurous cyclist
40–60km (25–40 miles)

challenging full-day rides
over 60km (over 40 miles)

grande randonnée – a grand cycling tour
100km (60 miles)

Routes marked with this symbol are off-road or have off-road sections
(includes well-surfaced cycleways as well as rougher off-road tracks)

The Cheviot Hills

LOCATION MAP 

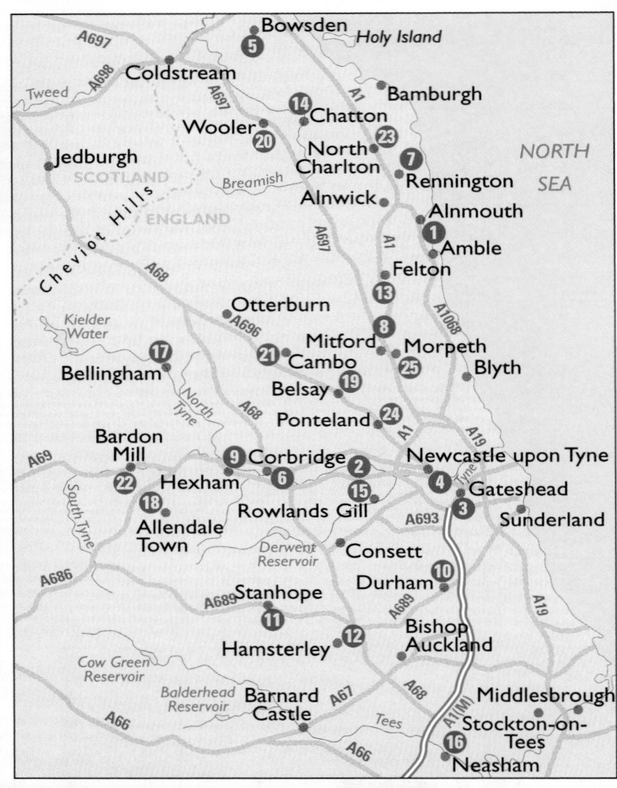

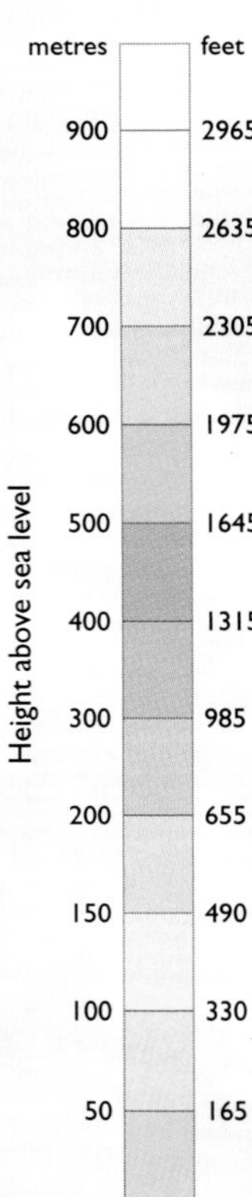

KEY TO ROUTE MAPS 

M23 Service area — Motorway

A259 — 'A' road / Dual carriageway

B2130 — 'B' road / Dual carriageway

Good minor road

Minor road

Track / bridleway

Railway / station

Canal / river

Lake / loch

50 — Contour (height in metres)

Cycle route / optional route

Start of cycle route

12 — Route direction

B — Place of interest

Public house

Café / refreshments

Restaurant

Convenience store

i — Tourist Information Centre

P — Parking

Telephone

Picnic site

Camping site

Public toilets

Place of worship

Viewpoint

Golf course

Tumulus

Urban area

Woodland

INTRODUCTION

How to use this guide

Collins' *Cycling in Northumberland & North East England* has been devised for those who want trips out on their bicycles along quiet roads and tracks, passing interesting places and convenient refreshment stops without having to devise their own routes. Each of the 25 routes in this book has been compiled and ridden by an experienced cyclist for cyclists of all abilities.

Cycling in Northumberland & North East England is easy to use. Routes range from undemanding rides compiled specifically with families in mind to challenging full-day rides; the type of route is easily identified by colour coding (see page 5). At the start of each route an information box summarises: total distance (in kilometres/miles – distances have been rounded up or down throughout to the nearest 0.5km/mile and are approximate only); grade (easy, moderate or strenuous based on distance and difficulty); terrain; an average time to allow for the route; directions to the start of the route by car and, if appropriate, by train.

Each route is fully mapped and has concise, easy-to-follow directions. Comprehensive information on places of interest and convenient refreshment stops along each route are also given. Accumulated mileages within each route description give an indication of progress, while the profile diagram is a graphic representation of gradients along the route. These should be used as a guide only.

The following abbreviations are used in the route directions:

LHF	left hand fork
RHF	right hand fork
SO	straight on
SP	signpost
TJ	T junction
TL	turn left
TR	turn right
XR	crossroads

Cycling in Northumberland & North East England

The rides in this book run through north east England, covering an area from the Kielder Forest in the west to the North Sea coast in the east, and from Barnard Castle in the south to Wooler in the north, with a foray over the Border into Kirk Yetholm. The routes stay away from busy main roads as much as possible to allow cyclists to discover the peaceful back lanes, forestry tracks and cycleways that cross this area, passing all manner of museums, castles, historic houses and other attractions. There are steep sections to be tackled in some of the routes. This, however, is compensated for by spectacular views.

Various off-road routes are followed, including sections of the National Cycle Network and several railway paths. Be aware that these routes are often designated as multi-use, for walkers and horse riders as well as cyclists. The National Cycle Network is being developed by the charity Sustrans and will link urban areas with the countryside. The award-winning C2C (Sea to Sea) crosses northern England from Whitehaven or Workington to Sunderland or Newcastle. The Reivers Way also crosses the country, from Whitehaven to Tynemouth. For information contact Sustrans at 35 King Street, Bristol, BS1 4DZ, telephone (0117) 926 8893, www.sustrans.org.uk. The decline of industry has left many disused railway lines which have been developed into a network of easily accessible paths. For further information contact a Tourist Information Centre (see page 13).

Geology, geography and history

This part of northern England encompasses varied landscapes. The rolling hills of the Cheviots comprise volcanic granite, shaped by glacial activity during the Ice Age and today covered by heather moorland, rough grassland and forestry. The north Pennines, comprising limestone, sandstone and shale, are home to many small towns and villages, often built to house the workers of the lead mines that flourished during the 19th century. There are also cliffs, sand dunes and mudflats along the coast, and the valleys of the rivers North and South Tyne, the Tees, and their tributaries.

Hadrian's Wall was constructed between AD122 and 163, stretching 117km (73 miles) between the Solway Firth and Newcastle. In 410 the Romans left Britain, to be followed by Anglo-Saxon invaders. The arrival of St Aidan from Ireland during the 7th century heralded the start of Christianity in Britain. During the 8th and 9th

Newcastle upon Tyne

centuries, Northumberland was again invaded, this time by the Vikings. In 1066 the Normans invaded England, reaching as far north as the River Tweed. William the Conqueror's reign established a previously unseen unity in England, focussing attention on the English/Scottish Border. The border lands became the scene of continuous warfare and lawlessness. The distrust between the English and the Scots created an economy dependent almost entirely on theft. When James VI of Scotland succeeded to the English throne in 1603 he imposed peace on the area. Trade and industry became more important, with the huge growth of heavy industry during the 19th century. Today the economy depends mainly on agriculture, service industries and leisure and tourism.

Preparing for a cycling trip

Basic maintenance

A cycle ride is an immense pleasure, particularly on a warm sunny day. Nothing is better than coasting along a country lane gazing over the countryside. Unfortunately, not every cycling day is as perfect as this, and it is important to make sure that your bike is in good order and that you are taking the necessary clothing and supplies with you.

Before you go out on your bicycle check that everything is in order. Pump the tyres up if needed, and check that the brakes are working properly and that nothing is loose – the brakes are the only means of stopping quickly and safely. If there is a problem and you are not sure that you can fix it, take the bike to a cycle repair shop – they can often deal with small repairs very quickly.

When you go out cycling it is important to take either a puncture repair kit or a spare inner tube – it is often quicker to replace the inner tube in the event of a puncture, though it may be a good idea to practise first. You also need a pump, and with a slow puncture the pump may be enough to get you home. To remove the tyre you need a set of tyre levers. Other basic tools are an Allen key and a spanner. Some wheels on modern bikes can be removed by quick release levers built into the bike. Take a lock for your bike and if you have to leave it at any time, leave it in public view and locked through the frame and front wheel to something secure.

What to wear and take with you

It is not necessary to buy specialised cycling clothes. If it is not warm enough to wear shorts wear trousers which are easy to move in but fairly close to the leg below the knee – leggings are ideal – as this stops the trousers catching the chain. If you haven't got narrow-legged trousers, bicycle clips will hold them in. Jeans are not a good idea as they are rather tight and difficult to cycle in, and if they get wet they take a long time to dry. If your shorts or trousers are thin you might get a bit sore from being too long on the saddle. This problem can be reduced by using a gel saddle, and by wearing thicker, or extra, pants. Once you are a committed cyclist you can buy cycling shorts; or undershorts which have a protective pad built in and which can be worn under anything. It is a good idea to wear several thin layers of clothes so that you can add or remove layers as necessary. A zip-fronted top gives easy temperature control. Make sure you have something warm and something waterproof.

If you wear shoes with a firm, flat sole you will be able to exert pressure on the pedals easily, and will have less work to do to make the bicycle move. Gloves not only keep your hands warm but protect them in the event that you come off, and cycling mittens which cushion your hands are not expensive. A helmet is not a legal requirement, but it will protect your head if you fall.

In general it is a good idea to wear bright clothing so that you can be easily seen by motorists, and this is particularly important when it is overcast or getting dark. If you might be out in the dark or twilight fit your bicycle with lights – by law your bicycle must have a reflector. You can also buy reflective bands for your ankles, or to wear over your shoulder and back, and these help motorists to see you.

You may be surprised how quickly you use up energy when cycling, and it is important to eat a carbohydrate meal before you set out. When planning a long ride, eat well the night before. You should eat small amounts of food regularly while you are cycling, or you may find that your energy suddenly disappears, particularly if there are hills or if the weather is cold. It is important to always carry something to eat with you – chocolate, bananas, biscuits – so that if you do start fading away you can restore yourself quickly. In warm weather you will sweat and use up fluid, and you always need to carry something to drink – water will do! Many bicycles have a fitment in which to put a water bottle, and if you don't have one a cycle shop should be able to fit one.

It is also a good idea to carry a small first aid kit. This should include elastoplasts or bandages, sunburn cream, and an anti-histamine in case you are stung by a passing insect.

It is a good idea to have a pannier to carry all these items. Some fit on the handlebars, some to the back of the seat and some onto a back rack. For a day's ride you probably won't need a lot of carrying capacity, but it is better to carry items in a pannier rather than in a rucksack on your back. Pack items that you are carrying carefully – loose items can be dangerous.

Getting to the start of the ride

If you are lucky you will be able to cycle to the start of the ride, but often transport is necessary. If you travel there by train, some sprinter services carry two bicycles without prior booking. Other services carry bicycles free in off-peak periods, but check the details with your local station. Alternatively, you could use your car – it may be possible to get a bike in the back of a hatchback if you take out the front wheel. There are inexpensive, easily fitted car racks which carry bicycles safely. Your local cycle store will be able to supply one to suit you.

Cycling on-road

Cycling on back roads is a delight with quiet lanes, interesting villages, good views and a smooth easy surface to coast along on. The cycle rides in this book are mainly on quiet roads but you sometimes cross busy roads or have stretches on B roads, and whatever sort of road you are on it is essential to ride safely. Always be aware of the possibility or existence of other traffic. Glance behind regularly, signal before you turn or change lane, and keep to the left. If there are motorists around, make sure that they have seen you before you cross their path. Cycling can be dangerous if you are competing for space with motor vehicles, many of which seem to have difficulty in seeing cyclists. When drivers are coming out of side roads, catch their eye before you ride in front of them.

You will find that many roads have potholes and uneven edges. They are much more difficult to

Alnwick Castle

spot when you are in a group because of the restricted view ahead, and therefore warnings need to be given. It is a good idea to cycle about a metre out into the road, conditions permitting, so that you avoid the worst of the uneven surfaces and to give you room to move in to the left if you are closely overtaken by a motor vehicle.

Other things to be careful of are slippery roads, particularly where there is mud or fallen leaves. Sudden rain after a period of dry weather often makes the roads extremely slippery. Dogs, too, are a hazard because they often move unpredictably, and sometimes like to chase cyclists. If you are not happy, stop or go slowly until the problem has passed.

Pedalling

Many modern bikes have 18 or 21 gears with three rings at the front and six or seven on the back wheel, and for much of the time you will find that the middle gear at the front with the range of gears at the back will be fine. Use your gears to find one that is easy to pedal along in so that your feet move round easily and you do not put too much pressure on your knees. If you are new to the bike and the gears it is a good idea to practise changing the gears on a stretch of flat, quiet road so that when you need to change gears quickly you will be ready to do so.

Cycling in a group

When cycling in a group it is essential to do so in a disciplined manner for your own, and others', safety. Do not ride too close to the bicycle in front of you – keep about a bicycle's length between you so that you will have space to brake or stop. Always keep both hands on the handlebars, except when signalling, etc. It is alright to cycle two abreast on quiet roads, but if it is necessary to change from cycling two abreast to single file this is usually done by the outside rider falling in behind the nearside rider; always cycle in single file where there are double white lines, on busy roads, or on narrow and winding roads where you have a restricted view of the road ahead. Overtake on the right (outside) only; do not overtake on the inside.

It is important to pass information to other members of the group, for example:

car up – a vehicle is coming up behind the group and will be overtaking;

car down – a vehicle is coming towards the group;

single up – get into single file;

stopping – stopping, or

slowing/easy – slowing due to junction, etc., ahead;

on the left – there is an obstacle on the left, e.g. pedestrian, parked car;

pothole – pothole (and point towards it).

Accidents

In case of an accident, stay calm and, if needed, ring the emergency services on 999. It is a good idea to carry a basic first aid kit and perhaps also one of the commercial foil wraps to put around anyone who has an accident to keep them warm. If someone comes off their bicycle move them and the bike off the road if it is safe to do so. Get someone in the party to warn approaching traffic to slow down, and if necessary ring for an ambulance.

Cycling off-road

All the routes in this book take you along legal rights of way – bridleways, byways open to all traffic and roads used as public paths – it is illegal to cycle along footpaths. Generally the off-road sections of the routes will be easy if the weather and ground are dry. If the weather has been wet and the ground is muddy, it is not a good idea to cycle along bridleways unless you do not mind getting dirty and unless you have a mountain bike which will not get blocked up with mud. In dry weather any bicycle will be able to cover the bridleway sections, but you may need to dismount if the path is very uneven.

Off-road cycling is different to cycling on the road. The average speed is lower, you will use more energy, your riding style will be different and there is a different set of rules to obey – the off-road code:

1 Give way to horse riders and pedestrians, and use a bell or call out to warn someone of your presence.
2 Take your rubbish with you.
3 Do not light fires.
4 Close gates behind you.
5 Do not interfere with wildlife, plants or trees.
6 Use only tracks where you have a right of way, or where the landowner has given you permission to ride.
7 Avoid back wheel skids, which can start erosion gulleys and ruin the bridleway.

Some of the off-road rides take you some miles from shelter and civilisation – take waterproofs, plenty of food and drink and basic tools – especially spare inner tubes and tyre repair equipment. Tell someone where you are going and approximately when you are due back. You are more likely to tumble off your bike riding off-road, so you should consider wearing a helmet and mittens with padded palms.

Local Tourist Information Centres

Alnwick
2 The Shambles, Alnwick
Telephone (01665) 510665

Barnard Castle
Flatts Road, Barnard Castle
Telephone (01833) 690909

Beamish
The North of England Open Air Museum, Beamish
Telephone 0191 370 2533

Bellingham
Main Street, Bellingham
Telephone (01434) 220616

Bishop Auckland
Market Place, Bishop Auckland
Telephone (01388) 604922

Corbridge
Hill Street, Corbridge
Telephone (01434) 632815

Craster
Car Park, Craster
Telephone (01665) 576007

Durham
Market Place, Durham
Telephone 0191 384 3720

Haltwhistle
Railway Station, Station Road, Haltwhistle
Telephone (01434) 322002

Hexham
Hallgate, Hexham
Telephone (01434) 605225

Morpeth
The Chantry, Bridge Street, Morpeth
Telephone (01670) 511323

Newcastle upon Tyne
City Library, Princess Square, Newcastle
Telephone 0191 261 0610

Once Brewed
Northumberland National Park Centre, Bardon Mill
Telephone (01434) 344396

Rothbury
Northumberland National Park Centre, Church Street, Rothbury
Telephone (01669) 620887

Seahouses
Car Park, Seafield Road, Seahouses
Telephone (01665) 720884

Stanhope
Durham Dales Centre, Stanhope
Telephone (01388) 527650

Wooler
Market Place, Wooler
Telephone (01668) 282123

Local cycle hire

Kielder Bikes
Kielder Castle, Kielder Forest
Telephone (01434) 250392

Leaplish Cycling Centre
Leaplish Waterside Park, Kielder Forest
Telephone (01434) 250312

Newburn Leisure Centre
Grange Road, Newburn
Telephone 0191 264 0014

Also the Bike Shop, Consett Bicycle Company, Cycle Logical, Derek McVickers Sports, Weardale Mountain Bikes and Yarm Cycles, see below.

Local cycle shops

The Bike Shop
16 St Mary Chare, Hexham
Telephone (01434) 601032

Consett Bicycle Company
62/64 Medomsley Road, Consett
Telephone (01207) 581205

Cycle Logical
37 St George's Terrace, Jesmond, Newcastle
Telephone 0191 281 8383

Derek McVickers Sports
23 Front Street, Consett
Telephone (01207) 592058

Tyne Valley Cycles
The Forge, Bridge End, Corbridge
Telephone (01434) 633363

Weardale Mountain Bikes
Frosterley, Hamsterley Forest
Telephone (01388) 528129

Yarm Cycles
10 West Street, Yarm
Telephone (01642) 784269

Route 1

BOULMER AND ALNMOUTH

Route information

Distance 16km (10 miles)

Grade Moderate

Terrain Gently undulating roads.

Time to allow 2 hours.

Getting there by car Park at Alnmouth station. The station is not in the village – it is on the A1068, Alnwick to Warkworth road.

Getting there by train The route starts at Alnmouth Station. Telephone (0345) 484950 for travel information.

From Alnmouth station, north past the RAF base to Longhoughton. The route then heads east to the coast and the fishing village of Boulmer. Then, on to Alnmouth village, before returning to the station. There are superb views of the Aln Estuary and Alnmouth Bay.

Places of interest along the route

A Boulmer
A fishing village with a disreputable past as the centre of a major smuggling operation. Northumbrian and Scottish smugglers would collect rum and gin from boats coming in here.

B Alnmouth
The picturesque village is built on a spit of land between the River Aln and the North Sea and served as the port for Alnwick, although there are claims the village dates back to 684. There are several small gift shops along the main street leading to the beautiful and unspoilt beach.

Route description

TR out of Alnmouth station and immediately TL (do not go over railway bridge but turn away from it, down hill to roundabout).

1 SO at roundabout, SP Alnmouth B1338. Almost immediately, TL beside telephone box, down Steppey Lane, SP No Through Road.

2 Cross River Aln, walking over footbridge, and follow path into Lesbury, emerging opposite church. TR onto B1339.

3 TL, SPLonghoughton/Embleton/Seahouses (1.5km/1 mile). Continue along Longhouton Road, passing RAF communications site.

4 TR at TJ and immediately TR, SP Boulmer/RAF Admin Site. Pass aeroplane guarding RAF site entrance. Continue towards Boulmer.

5 Arrive Boulmer (8km/5 miles). Follow road round to right (church on RHS/pub on LHS). Continue out of village and along this road.

6 TL, SP Foxton/Alnmouth/National Cycle Route. Follow this road into Alnmouth. Spectacular views of River Aln.

7 To visit Alnmouth village, TL at roundabout, onto main street and down to sea. After visit, retrace to roundabout where TL, SP Newcastle/Alnwick.

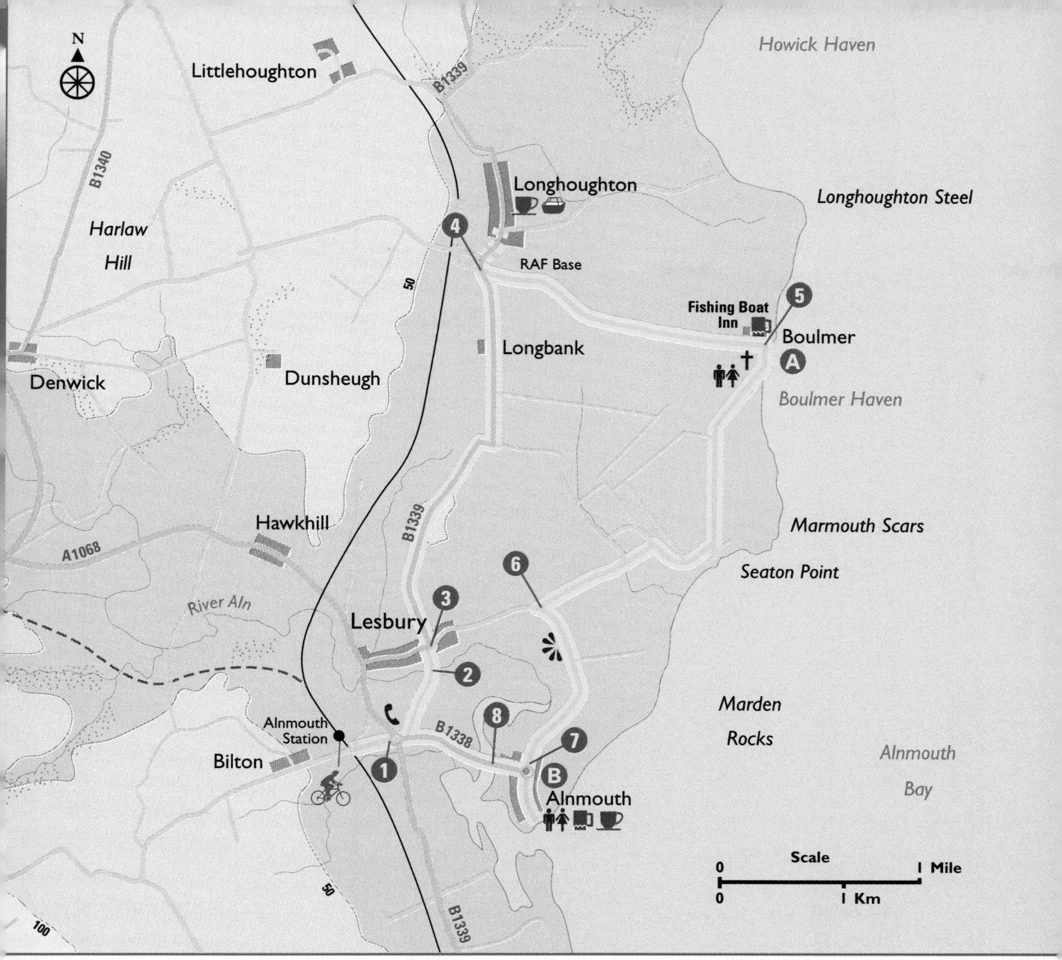

Otherwise, TR at roundabout, SP Newcastle/ Alnwick.

8 Cross River Aln. Continue to roundabout where SO. Continue up hill to finish route at station (on RHS). ***16km (10 miles)***

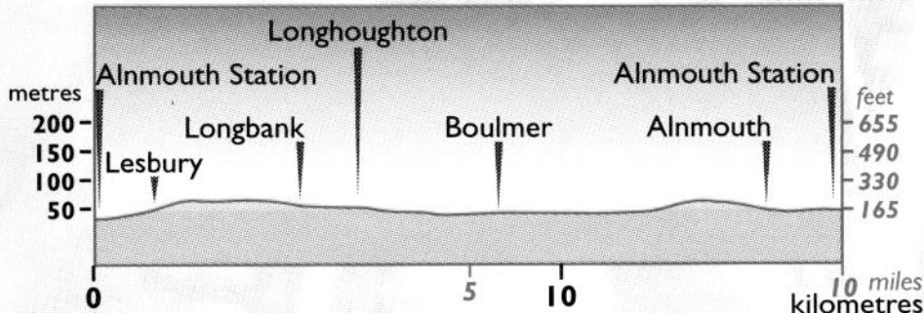

Food and drink

Longhouton has a shop and a basic NAFFI facility (not recommended), and there is plenty of choice in Alnmouth, including two tearooms.

Fishing Boat Inn, Boulmer

Open Tuesday–Sunday, 1200–1500 for sandwiches and drinks.

Route 2

THE TYNE VALLEY – NEWBURN TO OVINGHAM

Route information

Distance 19km (12 miles)

Grade Easy

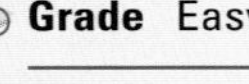

Terrain Flat, mostly off-road on good surfaces.

Time to allow 3 hours.

Getting there by car Tyne Riverside Country Park Visitor Centre is in Newburn, west of Newcastle. From the south, take the A695 over Newburn Bridge and TL past the leisure centre. From other points, turn off the A6085, past Newburn Leisure Centre, to the car park.

Getting there by train The Newcastle/Carlisle line passes through Wylam. Join the route in the station car park at direction 2. Telephone (0345) 484950 for travel information.

A figure-of-eight route, hugging the banks of the River Tyne. From Tyne Riverside Country Park at Newburn, the route crosses to the south bank of the river, to Ryton. Along to Wylam and then over to the north bank. On through the charming village of Ovingham, with its 17th-century houses, back across to the south side of the river to Hagg Bank Bridge, before returning through Wylam to Newburn. The Boathouse Inn, near Newburn Bridge, is marked with the recorded heights of some of the great Tyne floods.

Places of interest along the route

A Tyne Riverside Country Park, Newburn

Much of the park was reclaimed from derelict land during the 1980s. It extends over 81ha (200 acres) along the banks of the River Tyne. The Visitor Centre at Newburn offers information and displays on the park and its facilities. Telephone 0191 264 8501. Adjacent to the park is Newburn Leisure Centre where as well as swimming and other indoor sports, bicycles are available for hire. Telephone 0191 264 0014 for details.

B Wylam

A lovely village on the Gateshead/ Northumberland border. To the south is the river and the railway station. The station opened in 1835 and is one of the oldest still is use. **George Stephenson's Birthplace** (passed at direction 6) is a small stone cottage built c.1760 to accommodate four pitmen's families. The room in which Stephenson was born (1781), and in which the whole family lived, is open to visitors. National Trust property. Access by foot or bicycle only. Tea, coffee and cakes available. Open April to October, Thursday, weekends and Bank Holidays 1300–1730. Charge. Telephone (01661) 853457.

C Hagg Bank Bridge

An early example of an arch suspension bridge, built in 1876 at a cost of £16,000. Its design is similar to the Tyne and Sydney harbour bridges.

River Tyne

Food and drink

There are several pubs offering bar meals in Newburn and Wylam; also pubs in Ovingham (not open all day).

The Bakery, Wylam
In the village centre, the bakery has a small tearoom.

Adam and Eve, Low Prudhoe
Pub offering bar snacks.

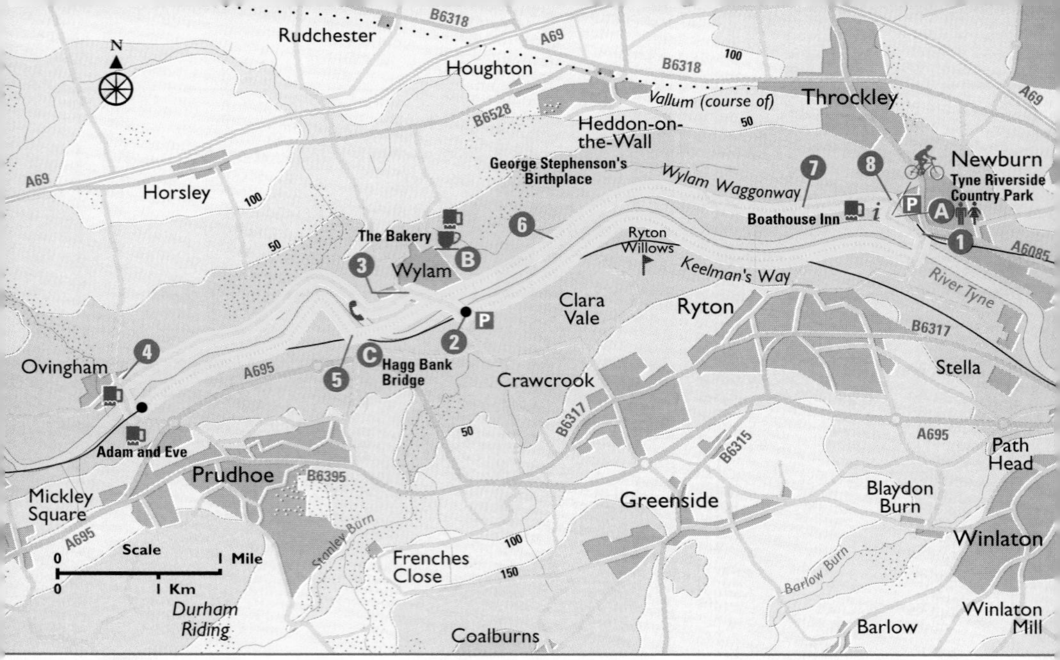

Route description 

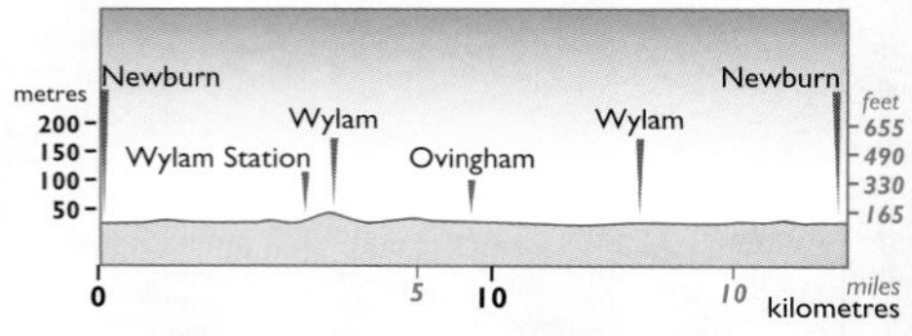

Start from car park at Tyne Riverside Country Park Visitor Centre. Join track alongside river, heading towards Newburn Bridge (river on your RHS).

1 TR over bridge at traffic lights. Immediately TR, SP Keelman's Way. Continue through Ryton Willows, skirting Ryton golf course (watch out for golf balls) and on through Wylam station car park. ***4.5km (3 miles)***

2 TR onto road and cycle over bridge into Wylam.

3 TL at TJ, SP Ovingham. Continue to Ovingham.

4 In Ovingham, TL over bridge (9.5km/ 6 miles) and immediately TR into Tyne Riverside Country Park. Join track alongside river (river now on your LHS). Continue to a telephone box on LHS (just past a terrace of houses).

5 TL then immediately TR down to and over Hagg Bank Bridge. Follow track through Wylam and onto Wylam Waggonway.

6 Continue SO, passing George Stephenson's birthplace on LHS.

7 Reach end of track and continue SO on road.

8 TR at TJ to return to the visitor centre car park and the end of the route.

19km (12 miles)

Route **3**

THE ANGEL OF THE NORTH AND BEAMISH

Route information

Distance 20km (12.5 miles)

Grade Strenuous

Terrain A hilly route along country lanes. The short off-road section is rough in places.

Time to allow 3–5 hours.

Getting there by car The Angel of the North is just off the A1, south of Gateshead. Turn off A167, following SP to the Angel, where there is parking.

Getting there by train There is no practical railway access to the route.

From the Angel of the North, the route descends into and then climbs out of the Team valley to Old Ravensworth. Following the ridge, the route drops down through woodland on an off-road track to Beamish. Then, back up to the ridge and down again into the Team valley, to finish with a climb back to the magnificent Angel.

Places of interest along the route

A The Angel of the North, near Gateshead

A wonderful, striking, award-winning sculpture, standing 20m (65.5 feet) high with a wingspan of 54m (177 feet). Created by Antony Gormley from 203,200kg (200 tons) of steel, this is Britain's largest sculpture and it has dominated the skyline since it was assembled on site in February 1998. Access at all times. Free. Telephone 0191 477 3478.

B Beamish Open Air Museum, Beamish

An award-winning recreation of Northern life around the turn of the century. The museum is set in 12ha (300 acres) and includes a town, farm, railway station and colliery village. Many of the attractions, including a terraced street, bandstand, Co-op store, school and chapel have been transported from local towns. Lots to do and see. There is a café (admission free) at the museum entrance and also one inside as one of the exhibits. Open Easter to October, daily 1000–1800; November to Easter, Tuesday– Sunday 1000–1700 (access to full site is limited in winter). Charge. Telephone (01207) 231811.

Food and drink

Refreshments are available at the Beamish Open Air Museum.

Angel View Inn, near Gateshead
Opposite the Angel of the North. Snacks and meals available daily.

Ravensworth Arms, near Lamesley
Meals served 1200–1430 and 1730–2100.

Shepherd and Shepherdess, Beamish
Close to the museum entrance. Open daily. Meals served with seating inside and out.

The Angel of the North

Route description

The route starts at the Angel itself. Follow path that starts under right wing, over open ground, through gate to TJ with road.

1 TL at TJ. Cycle down over A1 and railway line.

2 SO at roundabout

3 SO at junction, SP Sunniside. Then SO at XR.

4 TL, no SP (opposite SP Forest Enterprise Ravensworth). ***4.5km (3 miles)***

5 TL at XR, no SP, and SO past SP Bridleway.

6 TR at XR onto track, beside SP Sunniside/ Whickham. Follow this track to TJ with road.

7 TL at TJ onto the road opposite Beamish Hall (9.5km/6 miles). Continue SO, through Home Farm to mini roundabout – this is Beamish Museum entrance.

8 TL at mini roundabout (pass Shepherd and Shepherdess pub on LHS). Immediately

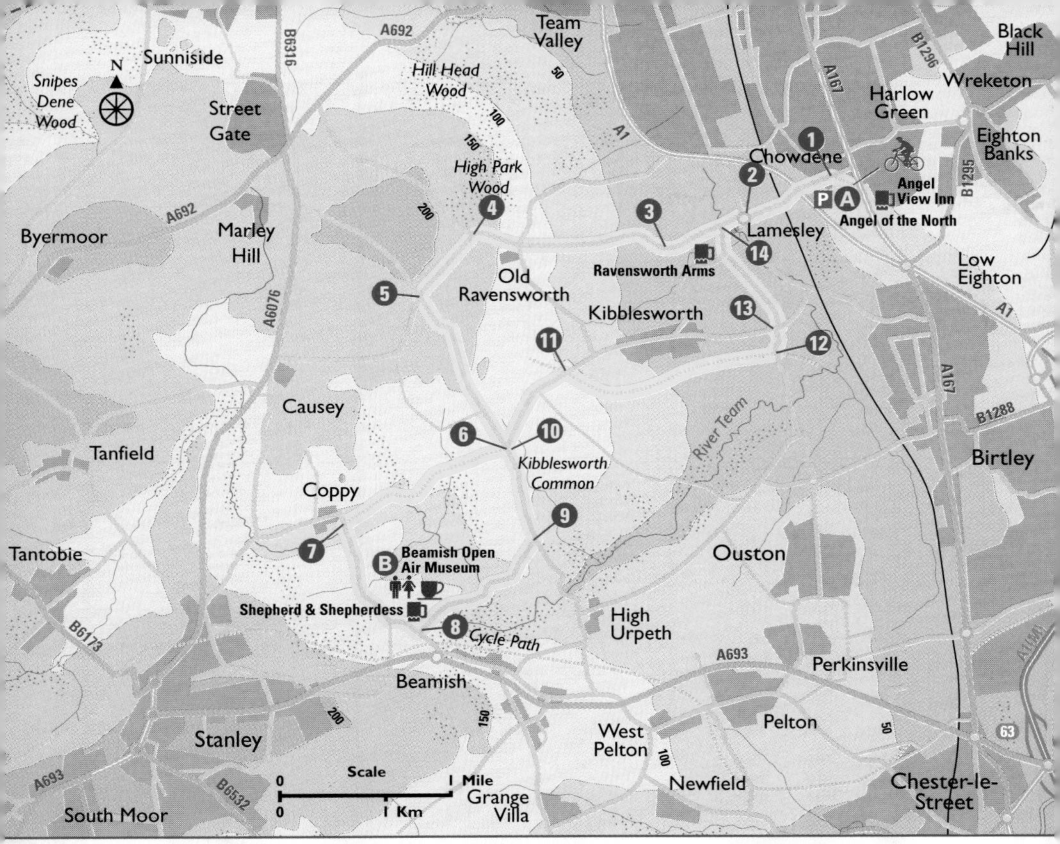

TL, SP Unsuitable for coaches. Continue SO, passing Bobby Shaftoe caravan park on RHS.

9 TL at TJ, no SP

10 TR along road at XR, no SP.

11 TR at XR with Bowes Railway Path and continue SO down hill on track. SO at XR.

12 TL at XR onto road, no SP.

16.5km (10.5 miles)

13 TR at TJ and immediately TL, SP Road Liable to Flooding. Continue SO and pass Ravensworth Arms.

14 TR at TJ, SP Lamesley. SO at roundabout and uphill to retrace route over railway line and A1. TR through gate and over open land to return to the Angel.

20km (12.5 miles)

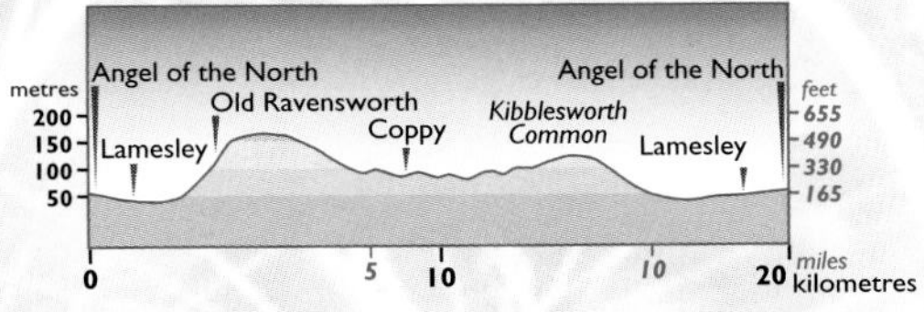

Route 4

DERWENT VALLEY RAILWAY PATH – NEWCASTLE TO ROWLANDS GILL

Route information

Distance 22.5km (14 miles)

Grade Easy

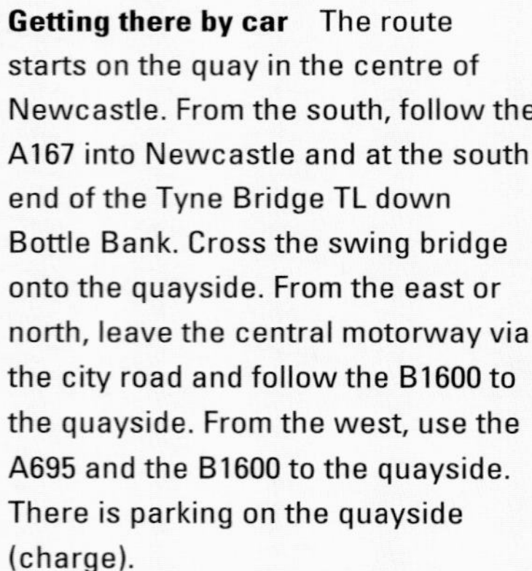

Terrain Mostly off-road, on level surfaces varying from muddy tracks to smooth tarmac.

Time to allow 2–4 hours.

Getting there by car The route starts on the quay in the centre of Newcastle. From the south, follow the A167 into Newcastle and at the south end of the Tyne Bridge TL down Bottle Bank. Cross the swing bridge onto the quayside. From the east or north, leave the central motorway via the city road and follow the B1600 to the quayside. From the west, use the A695 and the B1600 to the quayside. There is parking on the quayside (charge).

Getting there by train Newcastle railway station is 1km (0.6 miles) from the start. TR out of station into Neville Street and walk (against one way). TR into St Nicholas Street. TL at roundabout (underneath High Level Bridge) along The Close. TR at roundabout and follow road to Quayside.

A riverside route, starting on the quayside in the centre of Newcastle and following the Rivers Tyne and Derwent to Rowlands Gill, following a short section of the C2C and the Derwent Valley railway path. The railway opened in 1867 and at its peak carried half-a-million passengers as well as timber, bricks, coal and iron ore between Newcastle and Consett. The line was closed in 1962 and subsequently converted into a path for leisure use. The path crosses and recrosses the River Derwent on viaducts, offering wonderful views of the surrounding countryside and giving the cyclist an impression of Tyneside past and present, from the former industrial sites to today's modern landscapes.

Route description

Start on the quayside, with the swing bridge on LHS and the Quayside pub on RHS. Cross swing bridge via path on RHS. TR, SP Keelmans Way (with river on RHS). Follow this track under three bridges (High Level bridge, Queen Elizabeth metro bridge and King Edward railway bridge). As the track passes under fourth bridge (New Redheugh bridge) stay on it as it rises up away from the river to run behind a row of houses.

1 TR at TJ with road. Then SO at roundabout, passing gas works on LHS.

2 TR at TJ, no SP.

3 TL under railway bridge, SP Keelmans Way. Immediately TR onto track, SP C2C.

4 TL (just before foot/railway bridge across River Derwent) and go under road bridge (4.5km/3 miles). Take RHF to follow track beside river.

5 Continue under A1 and take RHF. Stay on this track, passing a footbridge on RHS.

6 TL onto tarmac and arrive at TJ with road. TL at TJ and immediately TR, SP Derwent Walk Country Park.

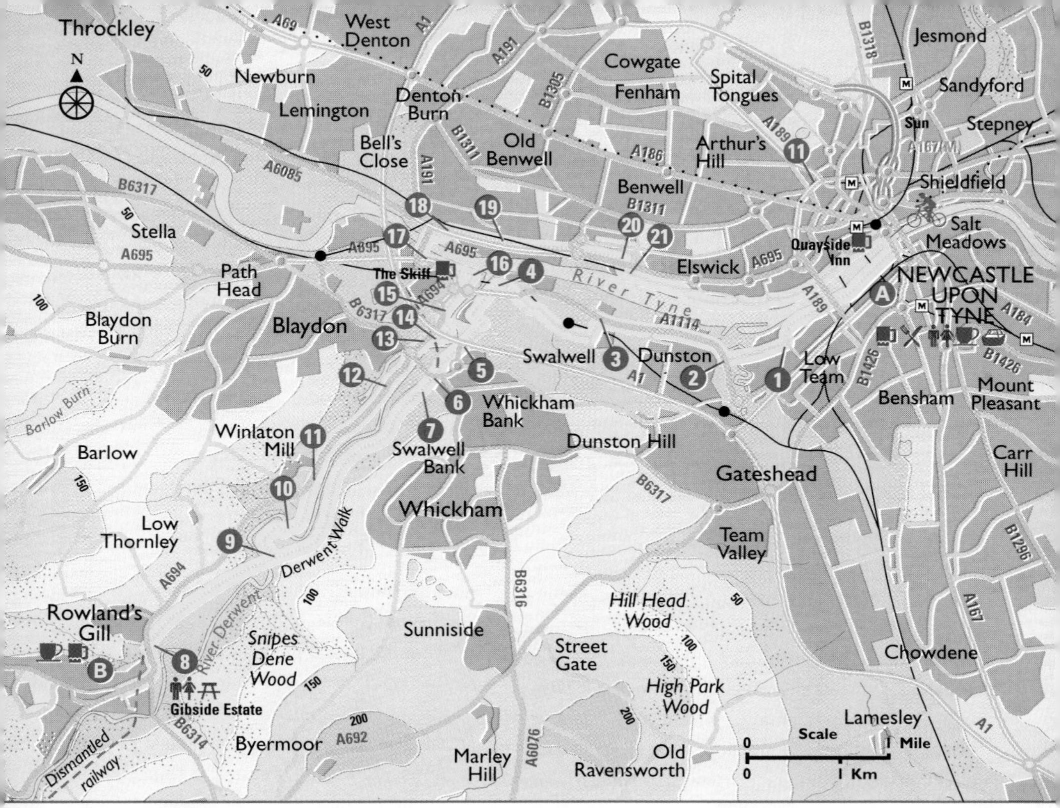

7 TL onto track (at gate SP Derwent Walk) and continue SO for a further 4.5km (3 miles).

8 TL off track onto path (11km/7 miles). Pass garage and enter Rowlands Gill. After visit, retrace route along Derwent Walk.

9 Cross viaduct and immediately TL onto tarmac path, SP Newcastle.

10 TL over wide bridge across river.

11 SO at XR, no SP.

12 SO at XR, SP C2C. Continue SO, with river on RHS and road on LHS.

13 SO at XR (road salt depot on LHS).

14 TR at TJ onto path (16km/10 miles), then TR SP C2C.

15 Take second TR at XR (red 14 discs on posts). Continue SO to river.

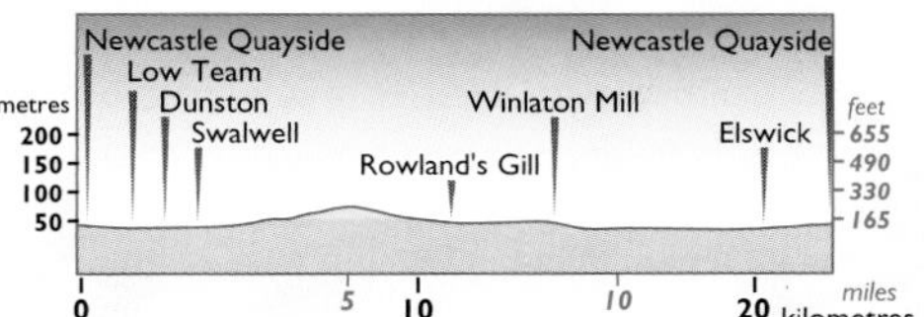

16 TL (river on RHS) and follow tarmac path alongside river, under road and foot/rail bridge. Where the River Derwent meets the River Tyne, LHF past Staithes and continue SO through Derwenthaugh Marina.

17 TL across grass to SP North Tyneside Cycle Way and go up ramp. Follow path over Scotswood bridge and continue round to right. Cross road via overhead foot/cycle bridge, SP Hadrian's Way.

18 TR, SP Hadrian's Way.

19 SO at XR. Continue SO following path as it drops down to join another beside road. SO, crossing Whitehouse Road, SP Hadrian's Way.

20 TR at traffic lights into Newcastle Business Park, SP Hadrian's Way.

21 TR onto path down to river (near bus stop), SP Hadrian's Way. Continue SO beside river and complete the route at the quayside.

22.5km (14 miles)

Places of interest along the route

A Newcastle upon Tyne

Newcastle has long been an important settlement: a Roman frontier station, the location of a medieval fortress and latterly a great port and centre for engineering and shipbuilding. Today Newcastle has many attractions for the visitor, with art galleries, museums, churches, monuments and, of course, great shops. **Castle Keep**, St Nicholas Street, is on the site of the new castle from which the city took its name. Built in 1080, the castle was originally constructed from wood and was entirely rebuilt from stone between 1168 and 1178. The steep climb to the roof affords visitors excellent views of the city, quayside and Tyne bridges. Open Tuesday–Sunday and Bank Holidays, April to September 0930–1730; October to March 0930–1630. Charge. Telephone 0191 232 7938. The quayside, at the heart of the city, has been revitalised. There are fine Victorian and Georgian buildings, a regular Sunday market and numerous restaurants and bars. **Bessie Surtees' House**, Quayside, is a 16th–17th century merchant's house, in what was the historic centre of the city. Bessie Surtees was the daughter of a banker who eloped and married in Scotland. The window from which she escaped is marked by a blue pane of glass. Open all year, Monday–Friday 1000–1600. Charge. **Trinity Museum**, Quayside, explores the maritime history of the River Tyne. Open April to October, Monday–Friday 1100–1600. Charge. Telephone 0191 261 4691. The **Riverside Sculpture Park** contains work by several different artists, some of it hidden amongst the trees. The park can be seen as the route passes under Redheugh Bridge. The Gateshead Art Map describes the park (telephone 0191 477 7454 to obtain a copy). As the route crosses the Scotswood Bridge, look down to the right to see armoured fighting vehicles manufactured on this site by Vickers. The final section of the route, alongside Newcastle Business Park, contains several sculptures together with information boards on the area's history.

B Rowlands Gill

Rowlands Gill is a former Victorian suburb of Newcastle, now a thriving community with a few shops, bank, pub and café. Nearby is **Gibside** Estate and Chapel, managed by the National Trust. The original hall was built in 1620; the grounds were landscaped by Capability Brown during the 18th century, when the chapel, designed by James Paine in the classical palladian style, and monumental statue to British Liberty were also constructed. Shop and tearoom. Chapel and grounds open April to October, Tuesday–Sunday 1000–1700; grounds only open November to March, Tuesday–Sunday 1100–1700. Telephone (01207) 542255.

Food and drink

Refreshments are available on the quayside, at the start of the route, and there is a pub and several cafés in Rowlands Gill.

The Skiff, by Scotswood Bridge
Bar meals available.

Route 5

FORD AND ETAL

Route information

Distance 24km (15 miles)

Grade Moderate

Terrain Undulating, quiet roads. The climbs are neither long nor steep.

Time to allow 2–3 hours.

Getting there by car The route starts at Bowsden. From the A1 northbound, take the B6353 through Lowick, then the B6525 to Bowsden. From the A1 southbound, take the B6525 through Ancroft to Bowsden. There is car parking near the village hall.

Getting there by train There is no practical railway access to the route.

From Bowsden to the ancient settlement of Lowick and then on to the twin model villages of Ford and Etal before returning to Bowsden. There is lots to see along the route, the highlight being Heatherslaw Mill and Railway.

Places of interest along the route

A Ford and Etal

The Ford and Etal Estate covers 6000ha (14826 acres) between the Cheviot Hills and the coast. Ford is a quiet hamlet built mainly by Louisa, Marchioness of Waterford and bridesmaid to Queen Victoria. The former school, **Lady Waterford Hall**, is decorated with her unique water-colour illustrations of biblical scenes. Open April to October, daily 1030–1230 and 1330–1730. Telephone (01890) 820224. Ford Castle, dating back to the 14th century is not generally open to the public (only to parties by appointment, telephone 01890 820257). Etal, twin estate village to Ford, is an attractive village with a pretty church and many thatched roofed buildings. Fourteenth-century **Etal Castle** (English Heritage property) contains an award-winning exhibition on Border warfare and the Battle of Flodden. Open April to September, daily 1000–1800; October daily 1000–1700. Charge. Telephone (01890) 820332.

B Heatherslaw Mill and Railway, Cornhill-on-Tweed

Heatherslaw corn mill is a working 19th-century water-powered mill. Visitors can see the miller at work. Also hand-on exhibits. Shop. Open April to September, daily 1000–1730; October daily 1100–1600. Charge. Telephone (01890) 820338. The Granary Café is adjacent to the mill and admission is free. The 15" gauge steam railway runs between Heatherslaw and Etal. The return journey of 4.5km (3 miles) takes 40 minutes. The trains carry bicycles (advance booking necessary) and could be used as an alternative route to Etal. Trains run April to October, daily. The first train of the day has a special rate for families. Charge. Telephone (01890) 820317 for information.

Etal church

Food and drink

Lowick has a post office, shop and café, as well as two pubs. A tearoom is sometimes open in Ford post office, otherwise the village is a good place for a picnic. Refreshments are also available at Heatherslaw Mill.

White Swan Inn, Lowick
Bar meals available at lunchtime.

Black Bull, Lowick
Well-known for its meals. Booking essential (01289 388228).

Post Office, Etal
Tearoom open Easter to September, Monday–Saturday (half-day closing Wednesday and Saturday).

Black Bull, Etal
Northumberland's only thatched roofed pub. Open daily, snacks available.

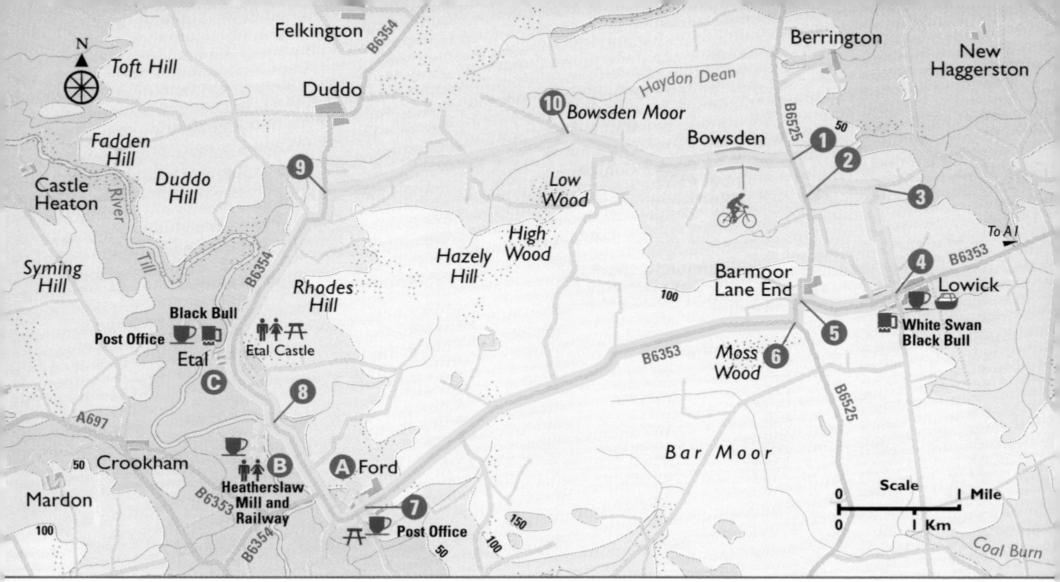

Felkington
Toft Hill
Duddo
Berrington
New Haggerston
Haydon Dean
10 Bowsden Moor
Bowsden
B6354
B6525
1
2
3
Fadden Hill
Castle Heaton
Duddo Hill
River Till
9
Low Wood
High Wood
Hazely Hill
Syming Hill
Rhodes Hill
Barmoor Lane End
To A1
B6353
4
Lowick
White Swan
Black Bull
5
Moss Wood
6
Black Bull
Post Office
Etal
Etal Castle
C
8
A697
Crookham
B
Heatherslaw Mill and Railway
A Ford
7
Post Office
Mardon
Bar Moor
Scale
0 1 Mile
0 1 Km
Coal Burn

Route description

Leave Bowsden heading east (village hall on LHS).

1 TR at TJ onto B6525, no SP.

2 Take first TL, SP Lowick Mill/Kentstone.

3 Take first TR towards Lowick, no SP. ***2.5km (1.5 miles)***

4 TR at XR in Lowick. Continue through Lowick, passing Black Bull pub on LHS.

5 TL at TJ onto B6265, SP Wooler/Ford/Coldstream. ***5.5km (3.5 miles)***

6 TR onto B6353, SP Ford/Coldstream. Continue to Ford.

7 TR into Ford, following brown tourist SP (12km/7.5 miles). After visit, retrace to B6353 and continue descent, passing Ford Castle gates on RHS.

8 To visit mill/railway, TL at bottom of hill, SP Heatherslaw Mill/Light Railway (14.5km/9 miles). The railway is immediately left; the mill and café are over narrow metal bridge on left.

Otherwise, continue SO through Etal, passing Etal Castle on RHS.

9 TR onto minor road, SP Gatherick/Bowsden, and continue.

10 TR at TJ, SP Bowsden/Lowick. Follow this road and descend to Bowsden to complete the route. ***24km (15 miles)***

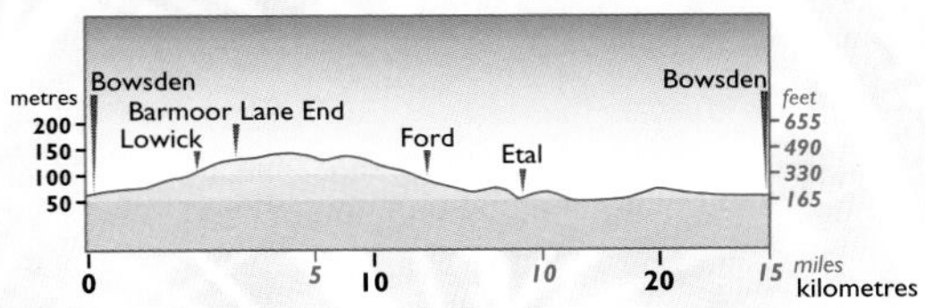

Route 6

CORBRIDGE, HADRIAN'S WALL AND AYDON CASTLE

Route information

Distance 24km (15 miles)

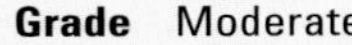

Grade Moderate

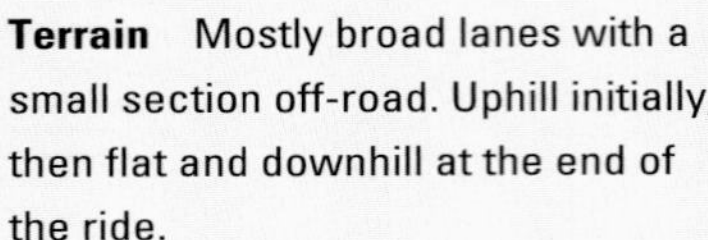

Terrain Mostly broad lanes with a small section off-road. Uphill initially, then flat and downhill at the end of the ride.

Time to allow 3–4 hours.

Getting there by car Corbridge is west of Newcastle, off the A69 (from the north or south, use the A68). There is parking in the village.

Getting there by train Corbridge railway station is south of the village centre. TR out of the station to the roundabout, where TR to cross the river into the village. Telephone (0345) 484950 for travel information.

A short and interesting circuit, with the uphill section over first. The route heads north east from Corbridge to Matfen, crossing the course of Hadrian's Wall twice. The visits to Aydon Castle and Halton add 6.5km (4 miles) to the total distance, but are recommended.

Route description

Start in Corbridge, opposite the Tourist Information Centre. Follow road out of Corbridge, SP Aydon, passing Golden Lion pub on corner. Continue past Aydon.

1 To visit Aydon Castle and Halton, TL, SP Aydon Castle/Halton.

Otherwise, continue SO to XR where TL.

2 TL at TJ with B6318, then immediately TR. Continue on this road.

3 To visit Matfen, TL at TJ (9km/5.5 miles) and continue to village.

Otherwise, continue and TL at next junction (10.5km/6.5 miles) Pass castellated house and standing stone.

4 TR at TJ, SP Stamfordham. Continue on this road.

5 TR onto track, SP Bridleway Great Northern Reservoirs. Follow track through farmyard (to left).

6 TR at TJ onto B6309. Then, SO at XR, SP Stocksfield.

7 Take RHF, leaving B road (16.5km/ 10.5 miles). Continue SO at XR and at next two junctions.

8 Take RHF (at third junction). TL at TJ onto B6321 and follow this road into Corbridge to complete the route. ***24km (15 miles)***

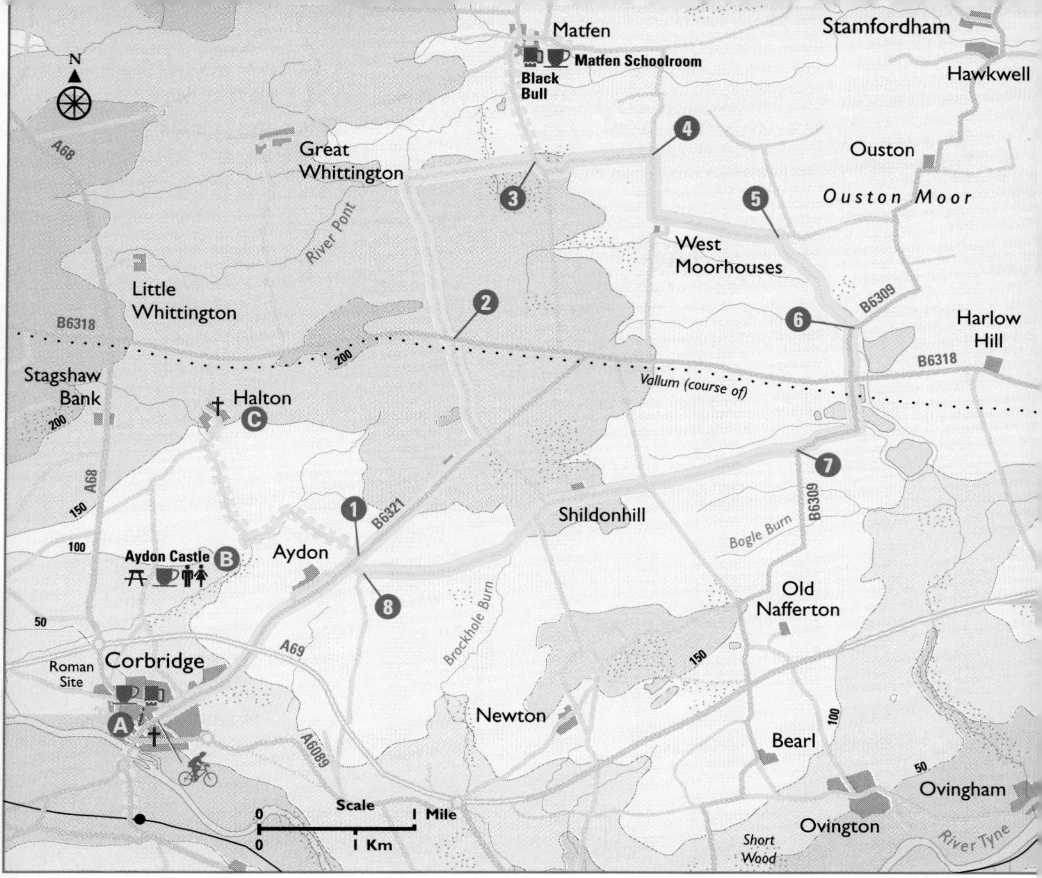

N

Matfen
Matfen Schoolroom
Black Bull
Stamfordham
Hawkwell
A68
Great Whittington
Ouston
Ouston Moor
River Pont
West Moorhouses
Little Whittington
B6318
B6309
Harlow Hill
200
Vallum (course of)
Stagshaw Bank
Halton
200
A68
150
B6321
Shildonhill
Bogle Burn
B6309
100
Aydon Castle
Aydon
Old Nafferton
Brockhole Burn
50
A69
150
Roman Site
Corbridge
Newton
A6089
100
Bearl
50
Ovingham
Scale
0 1 Mile
0 1 Km
Ovington
Short Wood
River Tyne

Food and drink 

There is a good selection of cafés and pubs in Corbridge.

Matfen Schoolroom, Matfen
Teas and snacks served in the old schoolhouse. Opening times vary, telephone to confirm on (01661) 886202.

Black Bull, Matfen
Bar meals available.

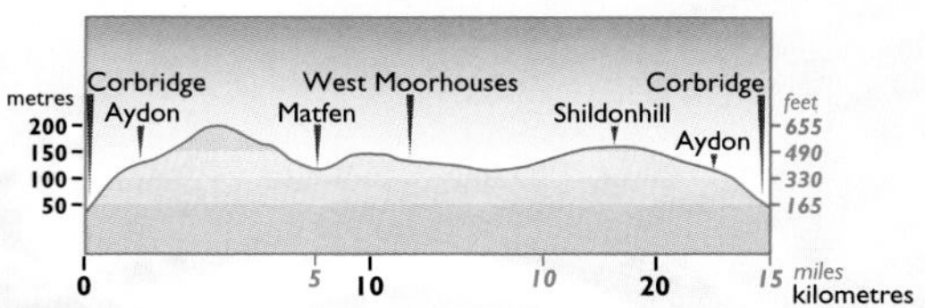

Places of interest along the route

Ⓐ Corbridge

Corbridge was an important Roman administrative centre, before becoming the capital of the ancient kingdom of Northumbria. The town has a 14th-century Pele tower, a good range of shops and a pleasant riverside area. **St Andrews Church**, Market Place, dates from the 7th and 13th centuries, with Saxon features. Open all year, daily dawn–dusk (except during worship). **Corbridge Roman Site**, on the Stanegate Roman road, pre-dates Hadrian's Wall. The extensive remains include granaries, strongroom, aqueducts and military compounds. Also museum. English Heritage property. Open April to September, daily 1000–1800; October daily 1000–1700; November to March, Wednesday–Sunday 1000–1600. Charge. Telephone (01434) 632349.

Ⓑ Aydon Castle, near Corbridge

One of the finest fortified manor houses in England. Aydon Castle was originally built as a manor house at the end of the 13th century and was later fortified. It is remarkably intact and displays many examples of original architecture. English Heritage property. A good place to picnic; refreshments available. Open April to September, daily 10000–1800; October, daily 1000–1700. Charge. Telephone (01434) 632450.

Ⓒ Halton

The castle and church are side-by-side. Although the castle is privately owned and not open to the public, it is worth viewing from the outside. The church of St Oswald, St Cuthbert and King Alfred is thought to be Anglo-Saxon. It is partly built of stones taken from the nearby Roman camps and wall (as are many stone buildings in this area). There are some interesting tombs and gravestones and a Roman altar. Near the church is an attractive green with a tiny duck pond.

Corbridge Roman site

Route
7

CRASTER AND DUNSTANBURGH CASTLE

Route information

Distance 31.5km (19.5 miles)

Grade Easy

Terrain Quiet roads and a small section of bridleway (concreted and suitable for all bicycles). There are two short climbs: one just after Craster village, the other after the bridleway.

Time to allow 3–4 hours.

Getting there by car The start of the route, Rennington, is 6.5km (4 miles) north east of Alnwick. Take the B1340 from the A1. There is parking in the village, near the village green.

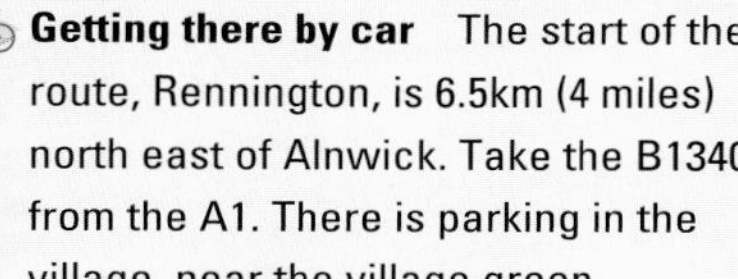

Getting there by train There is no practical railway access to the route.

From Rennington east to Howick and then north to the coast and Craster. Continuing north on a bridleway, the route passes close to Dunstanburgh Castle, and on through Embleton and Christon Bank. The route returns to Rennington via Rock.

Places of interest along the route

A Craster

This small fishing village and harbour, dating from 1415, is famous for Craster kippers and attracts lots of visitors. The harbour is at the centre of the village, and to the right are the kipper curing sheds. **Dunstanburgh Castle,** accessible by foot from Craster or Embleton, stands 305m (1000 feet) above sea level, high above steep cliffs. It was built by Thomas, Earl of Leicester in 1314 as a coastal defence against the Scots. The remains include the tower, which offers spectacular views. English Heritage property. Open April to September, daily 1000–1800; October daily 1000–1700; November to March, Wednesday–Sunday 1000–1600. Charge. Telephone (01665) 576231.

Food and drink

Bark Pots Café, Craster

Beside the Tourist Information Centre. Open daily with seating inside and out.

Jolly Fisherman, Craster

Opposite the kipper curing sheds, with a rear conservatory overlooking the dramatic coast. Sandwiches available.

Dunstanburgh Castle Hotel, Embleton

Open daily for lunchtime bar meals and evening restaurant meals.

Doxford Country Store, Doxford

Open daily for sandwiches and cakes, with seating inside and out. Also crafts, plants and a gallery.

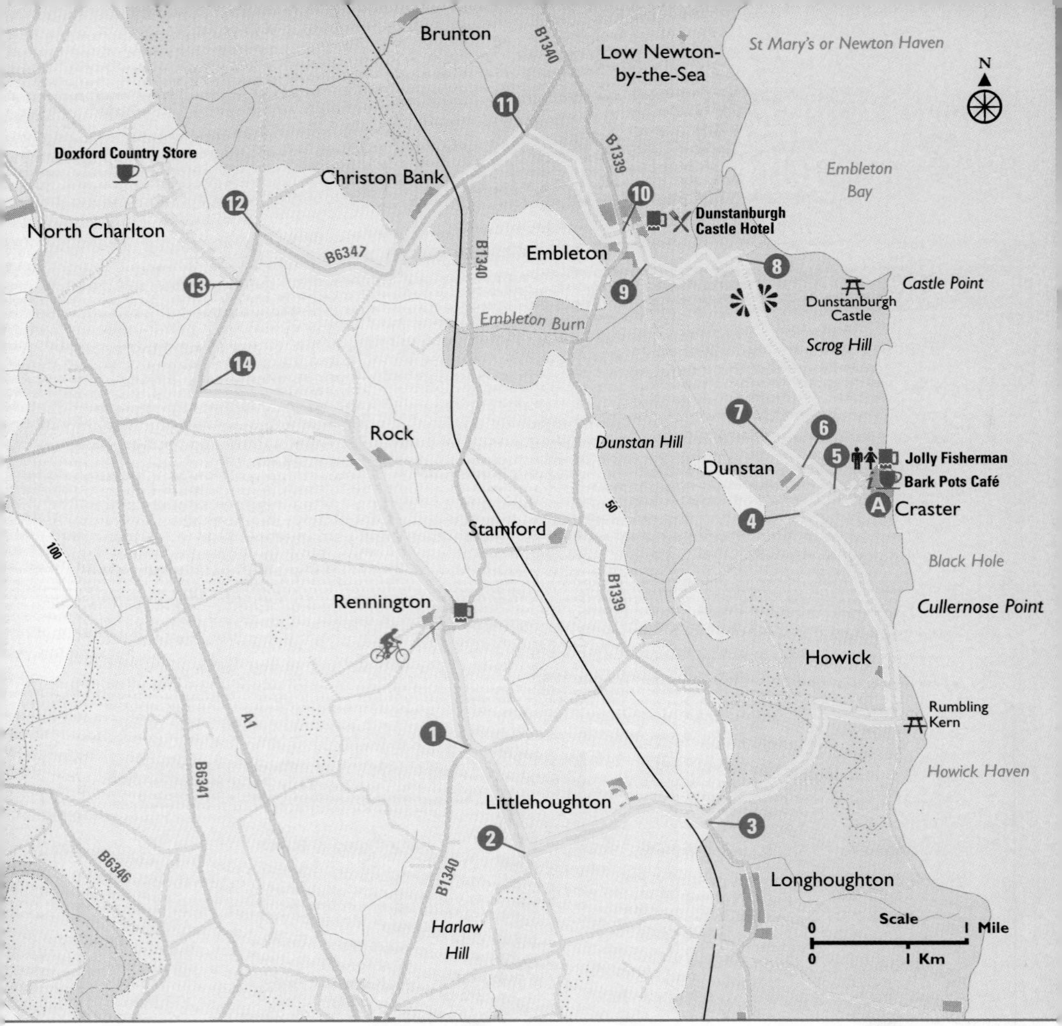

Route description

Leave Rennington heading south (village green on RHS, Horshoe pub on LHS). TR at TJ at end of village, SP Denwick/Alnwick.

1 TL, SP Craster/Littlehoughton and continue (ignore TL immediately after this junction).

2 TL, SP Littlehoughton/Howick. Descend over railway to B1399.

3 TL at TJ and then TR, SP Howick/Craster (4.5km/3 miles). Continue past Howick Hall and up to coast (where a five-bar gate directly ahead leads to Rumbling Kern, a super picnic place with small beach, only accessible by foot). Continue on this road towards Craster.

4 TR under stone arch, SP Craster.

10.5km (6.5 miles)

5 To visit Craster, TR at TJ. Otherwise, follow road round to left.

6 TR on corner, SP Embleton. Pass caravan site.

Dunstanburgh Castle

7 TR, SP Dunstan Square/No Through Road Except Cycles. Continue up past cottages and into farm yard. Join concreted bridleway (sea on RHS). Superb views of Dunstanburgh Castle and, on LHS, the Cheviot Hills. At end of bridleway, go through farm.

8 TL to join lane, cycling away from sea.

9 TR into Embleton at TJ (16km/10 miles). Follow road round to TJ (village hall on LHS/church opposite) where TR, SP Beadnell/Seahouses.

10 TL, SP Christon Bank. Continue out of Embleton village.

11 TL at TJ, SP Rennington/Alnwick. Go over railway and through Christon Bank.

12 TL at TJ, SP Rock/Doxford Farm/South Charlton/Alnwick.

13 To visit Doxford Country Store, TR and follow lane down and round to right. The store and gallery are in the courtyard.

Otherwise, continue SO.

14 TL, SP Rock/Rennington (27km/17 miles). Continue through Rock and back to Rennington. ***31.5km (19.5 miles)***

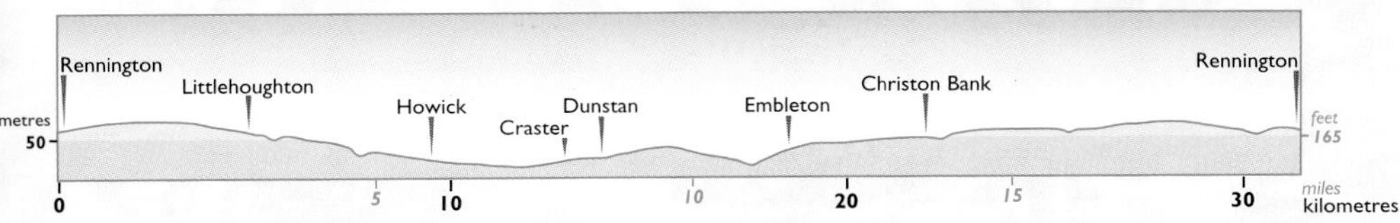

MITFORD AND BOLAM

Route information

Distance 33.5km (21 miles)

Grade Easy

Terrain Mainly flat road, with just a couple of short climbs.

Time to allow 3–5 hours.

Getting there by car Mitford is 4.5km (3 miles) west of Morpeth, on the B6343.

Getting there by train The nearest railway station is at Morpeth. To take full advantage of the gradients on the route, TR out of the station, down the hill and TL at roundabout. Pass golf club and TR onto B6354, SP Whalton. Pass the Searle Factory, go under A1 and TR, SP Mitford. Continue and follow route from direction 10.

From Mitford, alongside the River Wansbeck. The route then turns south to climb up past Marlish Farm to Bolam Lake Country Park. Then east through Bolam and Whalton, an exceptionally pretty village with a 12th-century church, before returning to Mitford.

Places of interest along the route

A Marlish Farm, Hartburn
A popular working farm, with over 300 animals to see and touch. Picnic areas, field and riverside walks, shop. Open mid-February to October, daily 1000–1700. Charge. Telephone (01670) 772223.

B Bolam Lake Country Park
Over 40ha (100 acres) of paths and bridleways, home to masses of birds and a few red squirrels. Information centre and picnic areas at the lakeside. Open daily, all year. Admission free. Telephone (01661) 881234 for further information.

C St Andrews Church, near Bolam
A charming church, noted for the Saxon tower and Norman chancelard, with an unusual war story – a bomb entered the church via a window casement but failed to explode, leaving the church intact. A window commemorates this event. Open all year, daily 0900–1700. Admission by donation.

Food and drink

The golf driving range at Gubeon has a café.

The Plough, Mitford
Bar meals available.

Dyke Neuk Inn, near Hartburn
Recommended for bar snacks and restaurant meals (telephone 01670 772662).

Stables Coffee Shop, Bolam West House Farm
Open Friday–Monday, 1030–1630.

Beresford Arms, Whalton
Bar snacks and restaurant meals available.

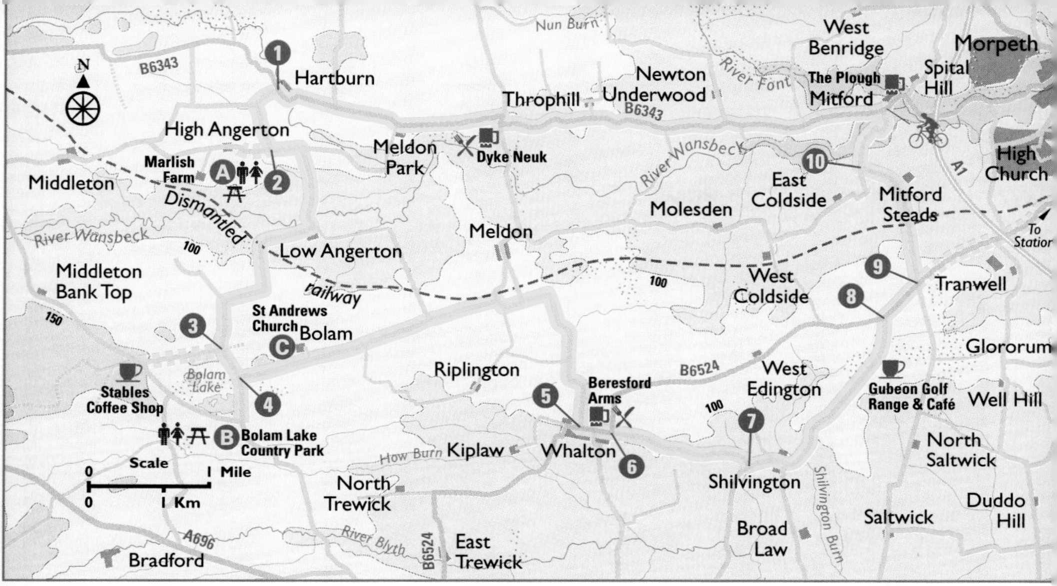

Route description

From the Plough pub in Mitford, leave the village heading west (pub on RHS, river on LHS). Continue on this road to Hartburn, passing Dyke Neuk pub and Meldon Park House/Gardens (limited opening, telephone 01670 772661).

1 TL in Hartburn, SP Angerton/Middleton (9km/5.5 miles). TL at next junction, SP Angerton.

2 To visit Marlish Farm, TR at TJ. Otherwise, TL at TJ, SP Angerton/Bolam.

3 Arrive XR. To visit Stables Coffee Shop, TR SP Scots Gap. Continue to XR where TR – coffee shop immediately on LHS.

Otherwise, continue SO, SP Morpeth/Bolam.

4 TR to visit Bolam Lake Country Park.

Otherwise, TL, SP Bolam (16.5km/10.5 miles). Continue on this road to Whalton, passing Bolam Church.

5 TL in Whalton and continue through village.

6 TR on bend (as road leaves east end of village), SP Shilvington. ***24km (15 miles)***

7 TL at TJ and TL again at next TJ, SP Morpeth. Pass Gubeon golf range/café.

8 TR at TJ onto B6524, SP Morpeth.

9 If you started from Morpeth station, continue SO and retrace route to station.

Otherwise, TL, SP Mitford. Spectacular views of Cheviot Hills on descent.

10 TR, SP Morpeth/Mitford (32km/20 miles). Pass Mitford church/castle and cross bridge into Mitford. TR at TJ to return to the Plough and the end of the route. ***33.5km (21 miles)***

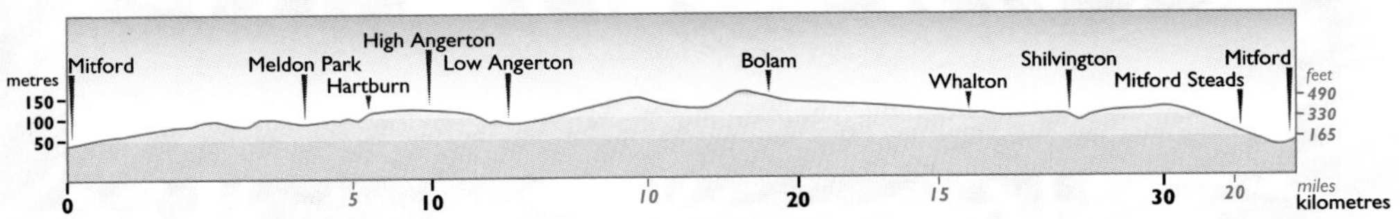

Near Blanchland

Route 9

HEXHAM, BLANCHLAND AND CORBRIDGE

Route information

Distance 40km (25 miles)

Grade Strenuous

Terrain Hilly, undulating roads through Slaley Forest and over Blanchland Moor; a descent and flat run along the Tyne Valley.

Time to allow 5–6 hours.

Getting there by car Hexham is west of Newcastle. Take the A69 and then the A695. Park in Wentworth car park (near Safeway supermarket), the start of the route.

Getting there by train Hexham is on the Newcastle/Carlisle line. For information telephone (0345) 484950. To reach the start of the route, TR out of the station. TL at the mini roundabout. Then TL into Wentworth car park.

From Hexham, heading south for a long climb out of the Tyne Valley. On along undulating roads to Slaley Forest for a steep climb onto Blanchland Moor and then down into Blanchard. The route then climbs back onto the moor, through the forest and across to Slaley. A last climb takes you up Prospect Hill before a descent into the Tyne Valley, through Corbridge and back to Hexham.

Places of interest along the route

A Hexham

A bustling town dominated by history and popular with visitors keen to explore nearby Hadrian's wall. **Hexham Abbey** was founded on the instruction of Queen Ethelreda in 674AD, but mainly dates from the 12th century and was built using stone from the Roman fort at Corstorpitum (Corbridge). Open daily, May to September 0900–1900; October to April 0900–1700. Admission free. Telephone (01434) 602031. The old goal was England's first purpose built prison but now houses the **Border History Museum** and Tourist Information Centre. The museum illustrates Border warfare of the 15th and 16th centuries, and the Jacobite rebellion of 1715. Open April to October, daily 1000–1630; November to February, Saturday, Monday and Tuesday 1000–1600. Admission free. Telephone (01434) 652349. The **Moothall**, a restored medieval building, houses the Border History Reference Library and a ground floor gallery, exhibiting local arts and crafts. Open all year, Monday, Tuesday, Thursday and Friday 1000–1230 and 1330–1500. Admission free. Telephone (01434) 601032.

B Linnels Bridge

A picturesque, narrow bridge over the Devils Water, built in 1581 by Wimfoira Erengton. Note the ants crossing back and forth on the parapet.

C Blanchland

A charming estate village built around a 12th-century monastery. The village is surrounded by hills and entered by crossing the bridge built by the monks. The Lord Crewe Arms was formerly a monastic building. Other buildings of note are the old gateway and the church of St Mary, a restoration of the original abbey church.

D Corbridge

Corbridge was an important Roman administrative centre, before becoming the capital of the ancient kingdom of Northumbria. See route 6 for more details.

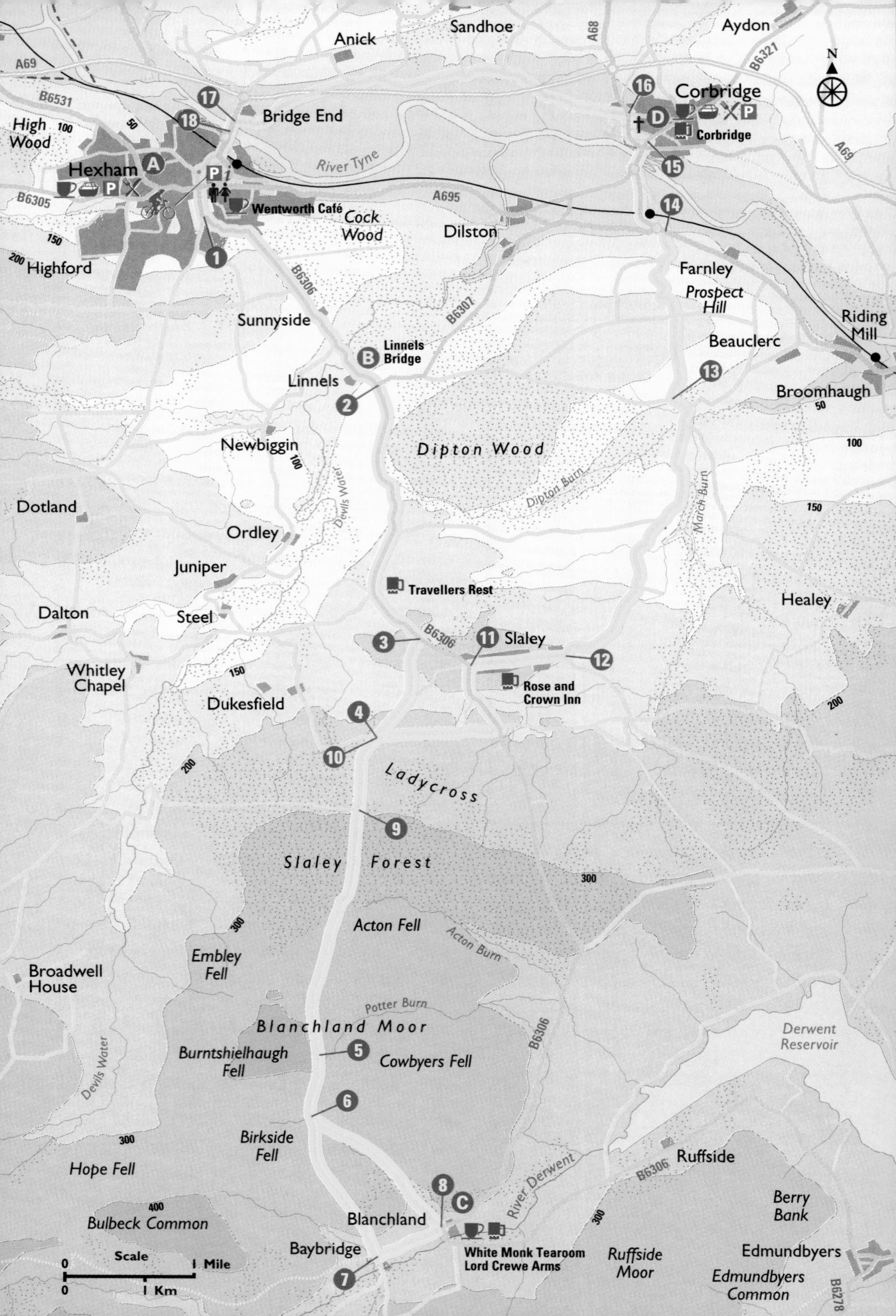

Aydon
Sandhoe
Anick
A68
A69
B6321
N
Corbridge
Corbridge
B6531
Bridge End
High Wood
Hexham
River Tyne
A69
B6305
Wentworth Café
A695
Cock Wood
Dilston
Highford
Farnley
Prospect Hill
B6306
B6307
Sunnyside
Riding Mill
Linnels Bridge
Beauclerc
Linnels
Broomhaugh
Newbiggin
Dipton Wood
Dipton Burn
March Burn
Devils Water
Dotland
Ordley
Juniper
Travellers Rest
Healey
Dalton
Steel
B6306
Slaley
Whitley Chapel
Rose and Crown Inn
Dukesfield
Ladycross
Slaley Forest
Acton Fell
Acton Burn
Embley Fell
Broadwell House
Potter Burn
Blanchland Moor
B6306
Derwent Reservoir
Burntshielhaugh Fell
Cowbyers Fell
Devils Water
Birkside Fell
Ruffside
B6306
Hope Fell
River Derwent
Berry Bank
Bulbeck Common
Blanchland
Baybridge
White Monk Tearoom
Lord Crewe Arms
Ruffside Moor
Edmundbyers
Edmundbyers Common
B6278
Scale
0
1 Mile
0
1 Km

Corbridge

Route description

Start from Wentworth car park. Take pedestrian exit (between public toilets and Wentworth Café), SP Tourist Information. Pass Tourist Information Centre/Border Museum on RHS. TL through Moot Hall arch. Then TL and walk bicycle to end of pedestrianised Fore Street. Take RHF, cross road and follow road, SP Blanchland.

1 Take LHF onto B6306, SP Blanchland, for steep climb and descent to and over Linnels Bridge.

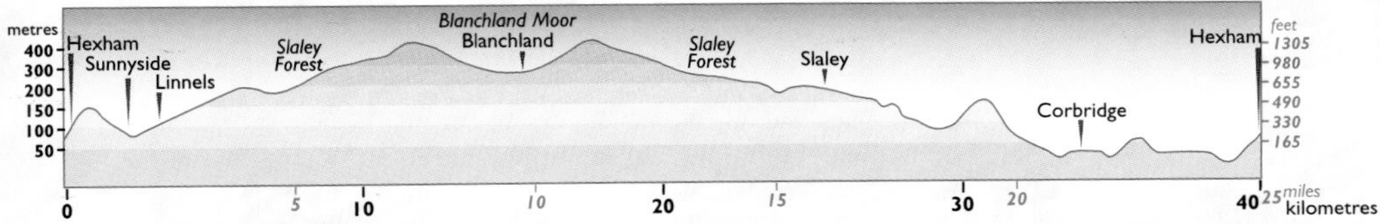

2 Continue SO, passing Travellers Rest Inn on LHS.

3 TR, SP Ladycross. ***6.5km (4 miles)***

4 SO at XR, SP Ladycross, and uphill through Slaley Forest. Continue, leaving tarmac road onto track at the edge of forest. Go through gate to cross Blanchland Estate on bridleway.

5 SO through two gates.

6 TR, SP Baybridge (just before third gate). Continue SO and pass through gate onto tarmac for descent.

7 TL at TJ, no SP. Continue into Blanchland.

8 TL at XR, SP Give Way, (16km/10 miles). Continue SO and uphill, off tarmac onto track. At gate SO, SP Ladycross. Retrace route through gates and over common to Slaley Forest.

9 SO at gate, back down hill through forest to XR.

10 TR, no SP. TL at next XR, SP Slaley.

11 TR into Slaley (25.5km/16 miles). Then TL, SP Riding Mill.

12 TL, SP Prospect Hill.

13 TR, SP Prospect Hill. Then SO at XR, SP Corbridge. Continue down twisting road to TJ.

14 TL at TJ, no SP, and immediately bear right, SP Corbridge (32km/20 miles). TR at roundabout, SP Newcastle A69, over bridge into Corbridge.

15 Take second TL, SP Newcastle A69. Go through town centre, passing church on RHS.

16 TL at Trinity Terrace (just past bus stop). Continue on this road, going under and then over A69, to outskirts of Hexham.

17 TL at TJ, no SP. Continue and cross River Tyne.

18 SO at next two roundabouts, SP Tourist Information. TL, SP Parking/Town Centre, into Wentworth car park to complete the route.

40km (25 miles)

Food and drink

Plenty of choice in Hexham and Corbridge. There is a pub and tearoom in Blanchland and a pub in Slaley.

Wentworth Café, Hexham
Conveniently placed at the start and end of the route.

Travellers Rest, near Slaley
Passed on route.

Right: *Statue of St Cuthbert*
Far right: *Durham Cathedral*

Route 10

DURHAM, BINCHESTER AND BISHOP AUCKLAND

Route information

Distance 48km (30 miles)

Grade Easy

Terrain Mostly well-surfaced, level cycle tracks. The linking roads have some climbs.

Time to allow 3–4 hours.

Getting there by car Park at Broompark picnic site, in Stone Bridge, 4km (2.5 miles) west of Durham on the B6203. Start the route at direction 2.

Getting there by train Several companies operate rail services to Durham. Telephone (0345) 484950 for information.

County Durham has a network of tracks over disused railway lines and this route samples three of these. From Durham, along the Deerness Valley track, for a climb up Crook Bank (superb views), before descending to the charming village of Brancepath. Another climb up Page Bank, to Whitworth Hall, and the route joins the disused railway track towards Bishop Auckland. Turning onto quiet lanes, the route descends to Binchester Roman Fort, with superb views of Newton Cap Viaduct. With a final climb into Bishop Auckland, you return to Durham over the viaduct.

Route description

From the southbound side of Durham railway station, go down hill and TL to go under viaduct. TR at roundabout, then TR at lights and SO, SP Crook, on A690.

1 TR onto B6302 at Stone Bridge roundabout, SP Ushaw Moor/Esh Winning.

2 TL into car park (after railway bridge), SP Broompark Picnic Area.

3 TR at TJ of tracks, SP Deerness Valley Line/Ushaw Moor.

4 To visit Esh Winning, TR by white building/ Station Hotel on RHS (10.5km/6.5 miles). Otherwise, SO to XR with road in Waterhouses

5 TL at XR, to join road by Button Place Terrace/telephone box.

6 TL at TJ in Hamilton Row (by Black Horse Inn), left SP Crook, right SP Cornsay Colliery.

7 TL at top of hill (on bend just before SP corner).

8 Road crosses disused railway track as it enters Brancepath. To shorten route and return to Brook Park/Durham, TL. Otherwise, SO to continue route.

9 Arrive XR (Brancepeth Castle/church are straight ahead). TR WITH CARE, onto A690 towards Crook. ***18.5km (11.5 miles)***

10 TL, SP Spennymoor/Page Bank/ Whitworth Hall Hotel, and continue.

11 Pass Shafto's Inn on LHS.

12 Arrive at SP for Spennymoor village. TR into Whitworth Road car park and follow track, SP Auckland Walk.

13 Track divides (stile SP Footpath to Byers Green). Take RHF. ***26.5km (16.5 miles)***

14 Track meets road. TR and continue into Byers Green.

15 TL (at house just before church). Continue up straight road.

16 SO at XR, SP Binchester Roman Fort. Follow road down and alongside stream (views of Newton Cap Viaduct). Pass TL to Binchester Roman Fort.

17 Arrive up steep slope in Bishop Auckland market place (Tourist Information Centre/Stan Laurel Room straight ahead). To visit Auckland Castle, TL onto one way system. Otherwise, continue SO to end of North Bondgate (Queens Head pub on RHS).

18 SO at first mini roundabout.

19 TR, just before second mini roundabout, SP Toronto/Crook. Continue out of town on path at RHS of Newton Cap Viaduct, SP Toronto/ Crook. Note: the viaduct has been refurbished and is a busy road. Keep to the path on RHS.

20 TR at end of viaduct, SP Picnic Area. Continue through car park onto track SP Brandon/Bishop Auckland Walk/Durham.

21 Arrive Willington (where track crosses kerbed road). Cross road, through bollards and play area. ***37km (23 miles)***

22 Cross another road and continue (school on LHS) to emerge by library.

23 TR WITH CARE at zebra crossing onto busy A690. Almost immediately TL (before Quality Fare supermarket), SP Brandon/ Bishop Aukland Walk. Resume track and continue.

24 Arrive at former Brancepeth Station. Continue SO on track.

25 CARE as track emerges from steep valley. Take LHF.

26 TR into Broompark picnic area. ***48km (30 miles)***

To return to Durham station, TR from car park onto B6203. TL at roundabout onto A690. SO at first traffic lights, then TL at second traffic lights to viaduct and up to station to finish the ride.

Quebec
Esh
Langley Park
Bearpark
Frankland
Cornsay Colliery
Ushaw Moor
Hedleyhope Burn
B6301
B6302
Deerness Valley Line
Vennels Café
Durham
Broompark
Waterhouses
Esh Winning
East Hedleyhope
River Deerness
New Brancepeth
Brandon
Langley Moor
Shincliffe
Wooley Hill
Broom Hill
High Wooley
Meadowfield
Weather Hill
Stockley Beck
Stanley
Brancepeth
Brancepeth Park
Oakenshaw
Billy Row
Sunderland Bridge
Croxdale
Hett
Crook
Lingy Close
Page Bank
Tudhoe
Willington
River Wear
Shafto's Inn
Rumby Hill
Sunny Brow
Todhills
Byers Green
Auckland Walk
New Hunwick
Newfield
Spennymoor
Howden-le-Wear
Dean Bank
Hunwick
Beechburn Beck
High Grange
Bell Burn
Binchester Roman Fort
Middlestone Moor
Middlestone
Ferryhill
Kirk Merrington
Westerton
Witton Park
Escombe
Coundon
Chilton
Scale
0
1 Mile
1 Km
Low Etherley
Rosso's
Bishop Auckland
Coundon Grange
Rushyford
Windlestone Park
High Etherley
A167
A690
A177
B6300
A689
B6298
B6299
A688
B6288
B6286
B6287
B6282
metres
feet
Durham
Esh Winning
Waterhouses
Wooley Hill
Brancepeth
Page Bank
Byers Green
Bishop Auckland
Sunny Brow
Willington
Brandon
miles
kilometres

Places of interest along the route

Ⓐ Durham

The historic city of Durham is dominated by the magnificent **Durham Cathedral,** built by the Normans on the site of a Saxon church. The cathedral contains the tombs of St Cuthbert and the Venerable Bede, whose writings give an insight into early history. Open daily, January to April and October to December 0700–1800; May to September 0700–2000. Tower open all year, Monday–Saturday 1000–1500. Charge. Telephone 0191 386 4266. The cathedral was the powerbase of the powerful Prince Bishops of Durham. **Durham Castle**, adjacent to the cathedral, was founded in 1072 and was one of the few castle never captured by the Scots. Open daily, March to April and July to September 1000–1700. Charge. Telephone 0191 374 3863. There is much more to see in Durham, including the Museum of Archaeology, Crook Hall and the Botanic Gardens. Telephone the Tourist Information Centre for further information on 0191 384 3720.

Ⓑ Brancepeth

This attractive village was almost completely rebuilt in the 19th century. There is a castle and beautiful church, which escaped the victorian rebuilding. Brancepath is an alternative starting point for the route (start from direction 9).

Ⓒ Binchester Roman Fort

Founded in the first century ad, the fort was one of several built along the Roman Dere Street. The site includes the best preserved military baths in the county. Open Easter and May to September, daily 1100–1700. Telephone (01388) 663089 or 0191 3834212.

Ⓓ Bishop Auckland

Famous as the seat of the Prince Bishops of Durham and where Dere Street crosses the River Wear. Magnificent **Auckland Castle** is the official residence of the Bishop of Durham. The chapel and state rooms are open to the public. Castle open 1400–1700: May to June, Friday and Sunday; July, Thursday, Friday and Sunday; August, Wednesday–Sunday; September, Friday and Sunday; also Bank Holiday Mondays. Telephone (01388) 601627. The 300-hectare (741-acre) park is open all year, daily 0700–dusk. Admission free. Telephone (01388) 601627. Young Stan Laurel started his acting career in Bishop Auckland. The **Laurel Room**, Town Hall, celebrates his life and gives details of a Stan Laurel walk around the town. Open all year, Monday–Friday 1000–1600. There is much more to see in Bishop Auckland. Telephone the Tourist Information Centre for further information on (01388) 604922.

Food and drink

Plenty of choice in Durham and Bishop Auckland. There are many picnic spots along the tracks, particularly beside the rivers and steams. Esh Winning and Willington have shops and pubs.

Shafto's Inn, Whitworth Hall Hotel

Overlooking Whitworth Deer Park and Lake. Refreshments available all day.

Rosso's, Bishop Auckland

In the market place and recommended for reasonably priced home-cooked food, teas and coffees. Closed Sunday.

Vennels Café, Durham

In Saddler Street and popular with locals. Seating inside and out.

Route **11**

DURHAM DALES – STANHOPE TO MIDDLETON TEESDALE

Route information

Distance 49.5km (31 miles)

Grade Strenuous

Terrain Some steep, short rises and longer hills.

Time to allow 4–5 hours.

Getting there by car Stanhope is on the A689 west of Wolsingham. There is free parking in the Market Square and main street, adjacent to the shops, Tourist Information Centre and Dales Centre.

Getting there by train There is no practical railway access to the route.

From Stanhope, following the River Wear along Wear Dale. The route then turns south to Newbiggin, following the River Tees to Middleton in Teesdale, before heading north back to Stanhope. There are some hard climbs, but these are followed by lovely long descents giving spectacular views of Wear Dale and Teesdale, part of the beautiful Durham Dales.

Places of interest along the route

A Stanhope

Stanhope, the capital of Weardale, was founded on agriculture, mining and quarrying. The limestone quarries, now defunct, provided limestone for the steel works in Teesside and Consett and the limestone was also used on marginal land to increase productivity. **Stanhope Castle,** opposite the stone cross in the market place, is a mock medieval castle erected in 1798. It is predated by the 12th-century Stanhope Hall. The hall is not open to the public but, as the most imposing building in the dale, can be seen from Stanhope Burn Bridge to the west of the town. In the church yard, adjacent to the market square, look out for the fossilised tree stump **Sigillaria**, reputedly alive some 250 million years ago. The churchyard has some 13th-century coffins made of Frosterley marble. The **Durham Dales Centre** contains craft work shops, Tourist Information Centre, tearoom and Dales garden. Open March to October, daily 1000–1700; November to February, Monday–Friday 1000–1600, weekends 1100–1600. Admission free. Telephone (01388) 527650.

B High Force and Low Force, Teesdale

High Force, in a designated Area of Outstanding Beauty, is England's largest waterfall with a dramatic 21m (69 feet) drop over the Great Whin Sill. Access at all reasonable times. Keep to the main paths as the rocks are slippery and the current strong. Nearer to Middleton is Low Force and the Winch Bridge, dating from 1830 and thought to have replaced an earlier suspension bridge. The falls are an essential part of Teesdale, as are the distinctive white buildings of the Raby estate.

C Middleton-in-Teesdale

On the Pennine Way and the capital of Upper Teesdale. An early agricultural settlement, the town developed with the sudden rise in prosperity heralded by lead mining during the 19th century and much of the architecture dates from this period. The world's first co-operative

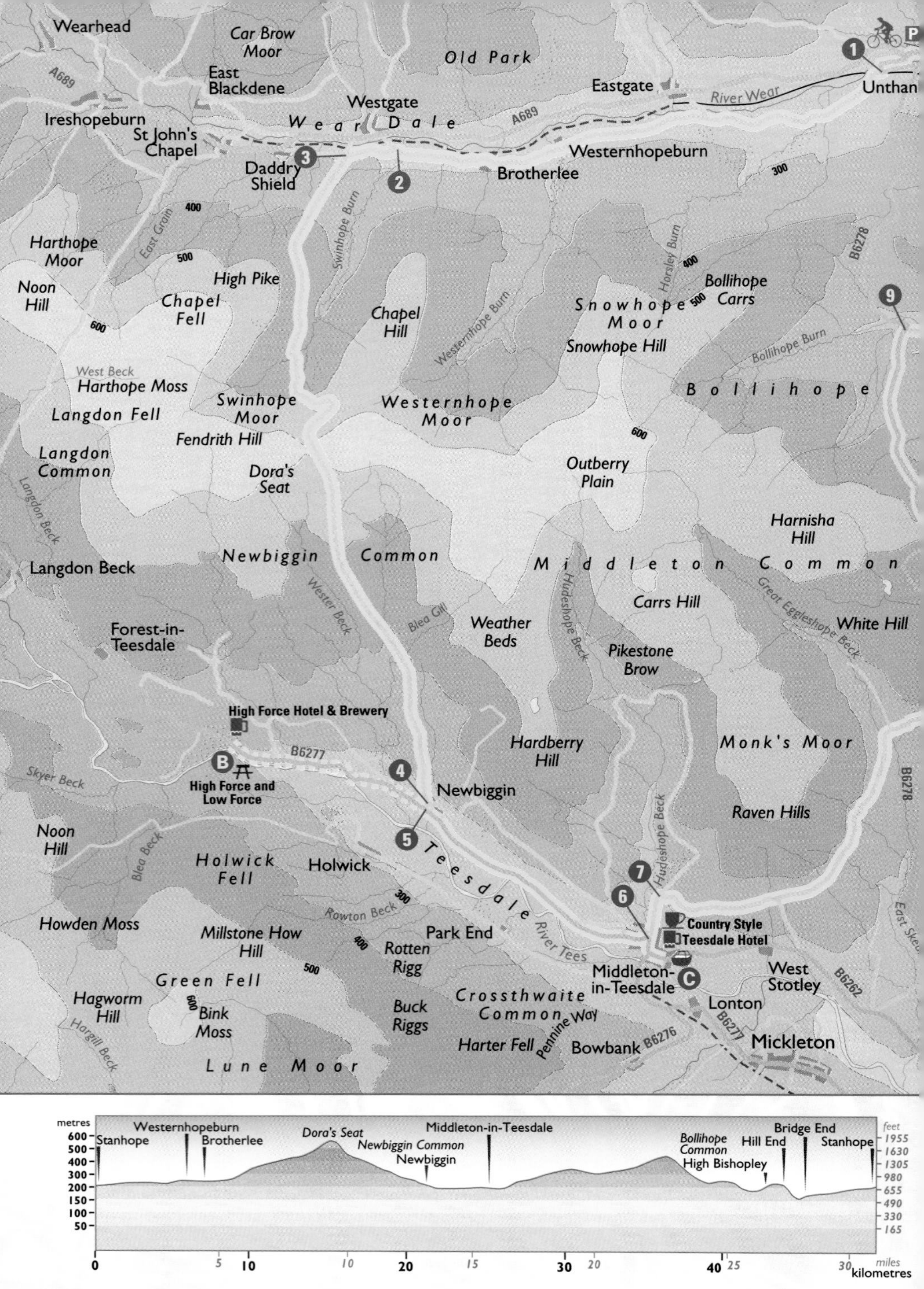

Wearhead
Car Brow Moor
Old Park
A689
East Blackdene
Eastgate
River Wear
Unthank
P
1
Ireshopeburn
Westgate
Wear Dale
A689
St John's Chapel
3
Westernhopeburn
Daddry Shield
2
Brotherlee
300
400
East Grain
Swinhope Burn
Harthope Moor
500
High Pike
Horsley Burn
400
B6278
Noon Hill
Chapel Fell
Chapel Hill
Snowhope Moor
500
Bollihope Carrs
9
600
Westernhope Burn
Snowhope Hill
Bollihope Burn
West Beck
Harthope Moss
Swinhope Moor
Westernhope Moor
Bollihope
Langdon Fell
Fendrith Hill
600
Langdon Common
Dora's Seat
Outberry Plain
Langdon Beck
Harnisha Hill
Newbiggin
Common
Middleton Common
Langdon Beck
Wester Beck
Carrs Hill
Great Eggleshope Beck
White Hill
Blea Gill
Weather Beds
Hudeshope Beck
Forest-in-Teesdale
Pikestone Brow
High Force Hotel & Brewery
Hardberry Hill
Monk's Moor
B6277
B
High Force and Low Force
4
Newbiggin
B6278
Skyer Beck
Hudeshope Beck
Raven Hills
Noon Hill
5
Blea Beck
Holwick Fell
Holwick
Teesdale
7
300
6
Rawton Beck
Country Style
Howden Moss
Millstone How Hill
Park End
Teesdale Hotel
East Skeer
400
Rotten Rigg
River Tees
Green Fell
500
Middleton-in-Teesdale
C
West Stotley
B6262
600
Hagworm Hill
Bink Moss
Crossthwaite Common
Buck Riggs
Pennine Way
Lonton
B6277
Hargill Beck
Harter Fell
Bowbank
B6276
Mickleton
Lune Moor
metres
600
500
400
300
200
150
100
50
Stanhope
Westernhopeburn
Brotherlee
Dora's Seat
Newbiggin Common
Newbiggin
Middleton-in-Teesdale
Bollihope Common
High Bishopley
Hill End
Bridge End
Stanhope
feet
1955
1630
1305
980
655
490
330
165
0
5
10
10
20
15
30
20
40
25
30
miles
kilometres

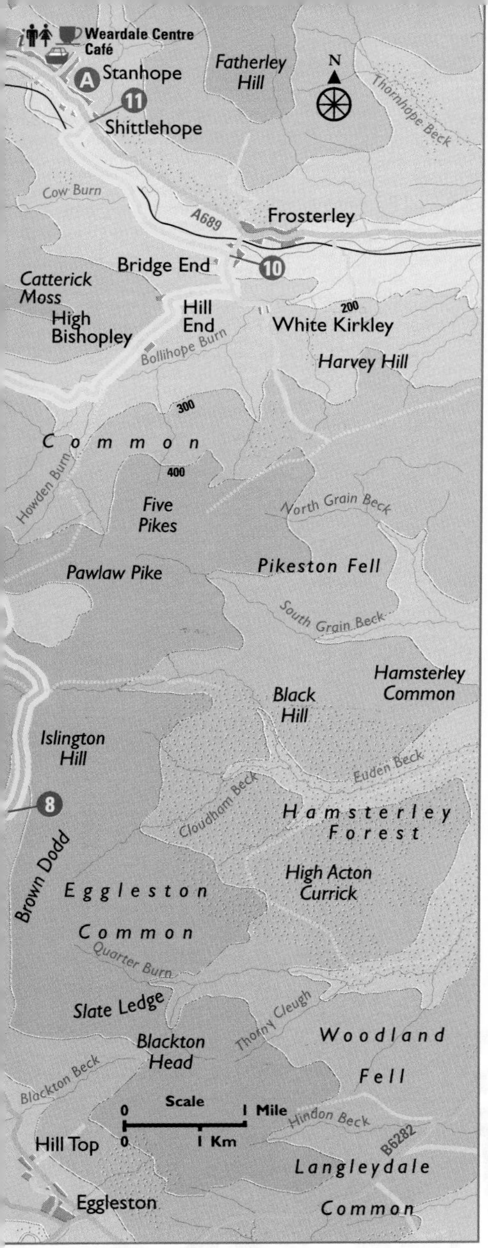

Weardale Centre Café
A Stanhope
Fatherley Hill
N
11 Shittlehope
Thornhope Beck
Cow Burn
A689
Frosterley
Bridge End
10
Catterick Moss
High Bishopley
Hill End
200
White Kirkley
Bollihope Burn
Harvey Hill
300
Common
400
Howden Burn
Five Pikes
North Grain Beck
Pawlaw Pike
Pikeston Fell
South Grain Beck
Hamsterley Common
Black Hill
Islington Hill
Euden Beck
Cloudham Beck
8
Hamsterley Forest
Brown Dodd
Eggleston Common
High Acton Currick
Quarter Burn
Slate Ledge
Thorny Cleugh
Blackton Head
Woodland Fell
Blackton Beck
Scale
0 1 Mile
0 1 Km
Hindon Beck
B6282
Hill Top
Langleydale Common
Eggleston

store was here, the Governor and Company's Teesdale Workmans' Corn Association, now the TSB bank building. There is an ornate Victorian drinking fountain in the main street and a 16th-century bell tower.

Route description

Start from Dales Centre, Stanhope and head west on A689 for 1km (0.5 mile). TL onto B6278, SP Eggleston/Barnard Castle/Teesdale High Force/Horsley Hall. Continue to and across bridge.

1 TR (after bridge) SP Horsley/Brotherlee/Haswicks. Continue on this road for 8km (5miles).

2 Take LHF, SP A689. ***9.5km (6 miles)***

3 TL and up hill at minor XR, SP 17% Unsuitable for Heavy Goods Vehicles (opposite SP Westgate via Ford). Go through gates at top and continue for approximately 11.5km (7 miles).

4 On descent through Newbiggin, take RHF to junction with main road (B6277).

5 To visit High Force/High Force Hotel, TR (an extra 6.5km/4 miles round trip).

Otherwise, TL (22.5km/14 miles) and continue to Middleton-in-Teesdale.

6 TL (after bridge on corner as you enter Middleton).

7 TR, SP Stanhope/Weardale, and continue on this road.

8 TL at TJ onto B6278, SP Stanhope (33.5km/21 miles) and continue.

9 TR, SP Frosterley/Wolsingham. ***40km (25 miles)***

10 On fast descent, TL before traffic lights and cross bridge (opposite Methodist Chapel), no SP, river on RHS.

11 TL onto A689 and return to Stanhope to complete the route. ***49.5km (31 miles)***

High Force

Food and drink

Convenience stores in Stanhope and Middleton-in-Teesdale (not open extended hours).

Weardale Centre Café, Stanhope
At the start and finish of the ride, open daily 1000–1700 daily, for good value home-cooked food.

High Force Hotel & Brewery, near High Force
Open all year, serving snacks and meals 1200–1430 and 1915–2115. Award-winning beer is brewed in the micro brewery on the premises. Accommodation available, telephone (01833) 622222.

Country Style, Middleton in Teesdale
Bakery and teashop open daily 0900–1700 (except Sunday Christmas–March), recommended to the hungry cyclist.

Teesdale Hotel, Middleton in Teesdale
The Stables Bar in the hotel is open for snacks: all day in summer; 1100–1500 in winter.

Route **12**

HAMSTERLEY, BARNARD CASTLE AND STAINDROP

Route information

Distance 51.5km (32 miles)

Grade Moderate

Terrain Well-surfaced roads, with some climbs.

Time to allow 4–6 hours.

Getting there by car Hamsterley is 19km (12 miles) north of Darlington. From Darlington take the A68 to Whitton-le-Wear and follow SP Hamsterley. There is car parking in the village.

Getting there by train There is no practical railway access to the route.

Hamsterley is well-known for the surrounding forest and common lands, popular with mountain bikers. Staying on-road, the route starts from Hamsterley and heads south to Barnard Castle. On past the Bowes Museum to Staindrop, before turning north back to Hamsterley.

Places of interest along the route

A Hamsterley Forest

The forest, planted around 50 years ago on land once used for lead mining, covers over 2,226ha (5,500 acres). The visitor centre contains displays on forestry and wildlife and provides information on activities within the forest (cycling, walking, orienteering and horse riding). Forest Enterprise property. Forest open all year, daily 0730–2100. Visitor centre open April to October, Monday–Friday 1000–1600, weekends 1100– 1700. Telephone (01388) 488312.

B Barnard Castle

A lively market town (market day is Wednesday), with many fine 17th-, 18th- and 19th-century buildings. The Butter Market marks the roundabout junctions of Thorngate, Newgate and Market, and dates from 1747, with a fire-bell crown. There has been a settlement here since at least Roman times, and the street Galgate stands on the line of a Roman road which crossed the River Tees by a ford upstream from the castle. The remains of **Barnard Castle** stand high above the River Tees. It was built by Bernard Baliol and Bernard's castle gave its name to the town that grew up around it. Dominated by an impressive round tower, the remains of the castle are extensive and impressive, and it is easy to see how this was one of northern England's largest Medieval castle. English Heritage site. Audio tour and gift shop. Picnics welcome. Open April to September, daily 1000–1800 (or dusk if earlier); October, daily 1000–1700; November to March, Wednesday–Sunday 1000–1600. Charge. Telephone (01833) 628212. The picturesque remains of **Egglestone Abbey** (English Heritage property) are open at all reasonable times, admission free. **Bowes Museum** was originally built by John Bowes, Earl of Strathmore, who made his fortune in the Durham coal industry. He married a French actress and together they amassed a great art collection. This is now displayed in this chateau and includes paintings, furniture, ceramics and tapestries. The surrounding 8-ha (20-acre) park is beautifully landscaped. Open all year, Monday–Saturday 1000–1730, Sunday 1400–1700; March, April and October closes 1700;

November to February closes 1600. Charge. Café (free admission) open April to October, museum opening times apply. Telephone (01833) 690606.

C Raby Castle, Staindrop

The Raby Estate covers large tracts of land north of the Tees and has distinctive white-painted buildings, many passed en route. The impressive castle is set in a 81ha (200-acre) deer park. Once the home of the Nevills, it has been owned by the Barnard family for over 370 years. It has an interesting walled garden, a collection of horse drawn carriages and, in the house, fine period paintings and furniture. Castle open 1300–1700: May and June, Wednesday and Sunday; July to September, Sunday–Friday; park opens at 1100. Charge. Telephone (01833) 660202.

Food and drink

There are cafés, pubs and hotels in Barnard Castle (extended opening on market day). Staindrop also has pubs and cafés.

Cross Keys Hotel, Hamsterley

Bar meals available.

Sun Inn, near Staindrop

Pub with a good reputation for bar meals.

Route description

Starts by Hamsterley village green. Head west, SP Barnard Castle/Woodland (Cross Keys pub on RHS). Continue on this road towards Woodland.

1 TR at TJ onto B6282, no SP (9.5km/6 miles). Pass Royal Hotel on RHS.

2 TL onto minor road, SP Kinninvie/Barnard Castle.

3 SO at XR, SP Barnard Castle.

16km (10 miles)

4 TL at TJ, SP Barnard Castle/B6278. Continue into Barnard Castle.

5 TR onto A67, SP Town Centre. Continue past castle.

6 TL at roundabout (Butter Market in centre), SP Whorlton/Bowes Museum. Continue to Whorlton, passing Bowes Museum.

7 TL at TJ, SP Alternative Route (blue SP).

27km (17 miles)

8 Arrive at XR with A67. SO, SP Newsham/Staindrop.

9 TL at TJ, no SP (31km/19 miles). Continue through Little Newsham into Staindrop.

10 TR at TJ, SP (back the way) Bowes Museum.

11 To visit Raby Castle, TL. To continue route TR onto B6279, SP Darlington.

12 TL by white barn onto minor road. Then TL at TJ.

13 Arrive TJ with A688 (41km/25.5 miles). TR, SP Bishop Auckland, and immediately TL, SP Cockfield (Sun Inn at this junction). Continue.

14 Take RHF then immediately SO at XR, SP High Lands.

15 SO at XR, SP Morley/Hamsterley.

16 TL at TJ, no SP but by bus shelter.

48km (30 miles)

17 TR at junction (after bend), SP Hamsterley. Continue back to Hamsterley and the end of the ride. ***51.5km (32 miles)***

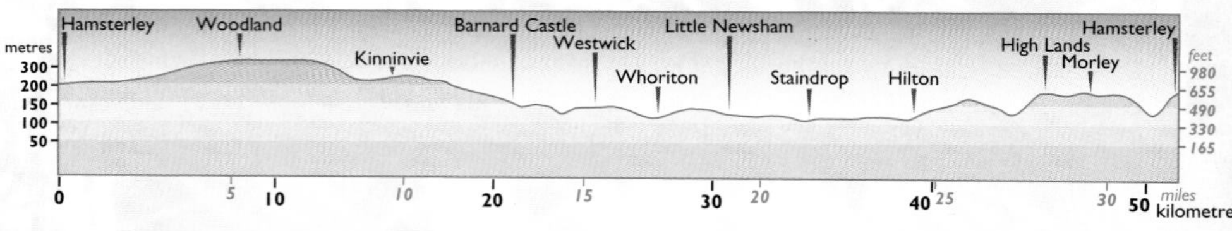

North Grain Beck
Cabin Hill
Harthope Beck
Mineral Line
A689
300
100
Bedburn Beck
River Wear
Witton-le-Wear
South Grain Beck
200
150
Bedburn
Cross Keys Hotel
Hamsterley
Ayhope Beck
Bedburn Beck
Hamsterley Common
Low Redford
Black Hill
Witton Park
A68
Euden Beck
Podgehole
Low Etherley
Linburn Beck
Hamsterley Forest
High Etherley
A
17
B6282
High Acton Currick
Spurlswood Beck
Toft Hill
16
Morley
A68
Woodland
1
Thorny Cleugh
B6282
15
Woodland Fell
Lane Head
Lynesack
High Lands
B6282
River Gaunless
150
Butterknowle
Evenwood
400
Copley
Low Lands
Cockfield Fell
Hindon Beck
300
Peathrow
Langleydale Common
2
Arn Gill
Penny Hill
14
Evenwood Gate
Cockfield
Crag Top
A688
Hollin Hill
Shotton Moor
Burnt Houses
200
200
Sun Inn
13
Wackerfield
Hilton
Kinninvie
Langley Beck
Raby Park
C
Raby Castle
3
B6279
B6279
12
B6278
150
11
100
Sun Inn
Staindrop
10
Sudburn Beck
Sudburn Beck
Langton
Langley
East Carrs Wood
4
New Broomielaw
Great Wood
Low Park Wall
Sainton
A688
Cleatlam
B6274
Gainford Great Wood
Dismantled railway
Black
Broomielaw
Beck
Beck
Little Newsham
5
9
Barnard Castle
Winston
B6277
Westwick Moor
8
Startforth
Bowes Museum
B
A67
Gainford
Arlaw Banks
A67
Whorlton
Beck
6
Westwick
High Close
Whorlton
East Shaws
150
River Tees
7
Ovington
Greystone
Boldron
B6277
Wycliffe
Scale
0
1 Mile
0
1 Km
Cross Lanes
A66
200
Caldwell
Gretna Bridge
B6274

Route 13

FELTON, DRURIDGE BAY AND MORPETH

Route information

Distance 54.5km (34 miles)

Grade Easy

Terrain Mainly on-road, with some moderate tracks and a few short climbs to allow close proximity to the sea. There is one brief stretch of footpath where cycling is not allowed.

Time to allow 3–4 hours.

Getting there by car Take the B6345 from the A1, SP Felton. There is car parking at the foot of the hill in Felton.

Getting there by train There is a railway station at Morpeth. Telephone (0345) 484950 for information. To join route, TR out of station, down hill. SO at roundabout, past police station to Tourist Information Centre where TL at roundabout to join route at direction 16.

From Felton, now bypassed by the busy A1, the route heads east to the coast and Druridge Bay Country Park. Turning south, the route follows the coastline to Cresswell. Heading inland, to Longhirst, a 19th-century estate village, and on to Morpeth, before returning north through typical Northumberland villages, to Felton.

Places of interest along the route

A Druridge Bay Country Park

The park opened in 1989 on land reclaimed from mining. When it was working, 2,731,574 tonnes of coal was extracted from the Coldrift opencast site. The country park now extends 4.5km (3 miles) along a stretch of the beautiful Northumberland coast and includes Ladyburn Lake. It is a conservation area popular for bird watching and for the grasses and flowers on the dunes. The visitor centre has displays and information on the local area and a café and shop. Open at weekends and during school holidays.

B Morpeth

Morpeth, the County Town of Northumberland, sits on the River Wansbeck. The 13th-century Chantry, in the town centre, is an old church building which now houses the Tourist Information Centre (telephone 01670 511323), a craft centre and the **Chantry Bagpipe Museum**, describing the history of Northumbrian pipes and music. Open all year, Monday–Saturday 1000–1700. Charge. Telephone (01670) 519466. Morpeth **Clock Tower**, Oldgate, dates from 1634 and contains bells dating from 1706, which still ring the evening curfew. To the south of the river, in **Carlisle Park** , a formal park containing the remains of Morpeth Castle, woodland and river walks and an aviary. Open all year, daily. Telephone (01670) 514351.

The Chantry, Morpeth

Food and drink 

Refreshments are available at Druridge Bay Country Park and there is lots of choice in Morpeth. Cresswell has a shop open during the summer selling cold drinks and home made ice cream.

Running Fox Café, Felton
Café and newsagent, beside the bridge. Limited seating but open daily for light meals and cakes.

Northumberland Arms, Felton
Meals available Wednesday–Sunday, lunchtimes and evenings.

Railway Inn, Acklington Market
Open Thursday–Sunday for bar lunches.

Old Bakehouse, Morpeth
In a courtyard on LHS side of main street going north out of the town. CTC approved and open daily.

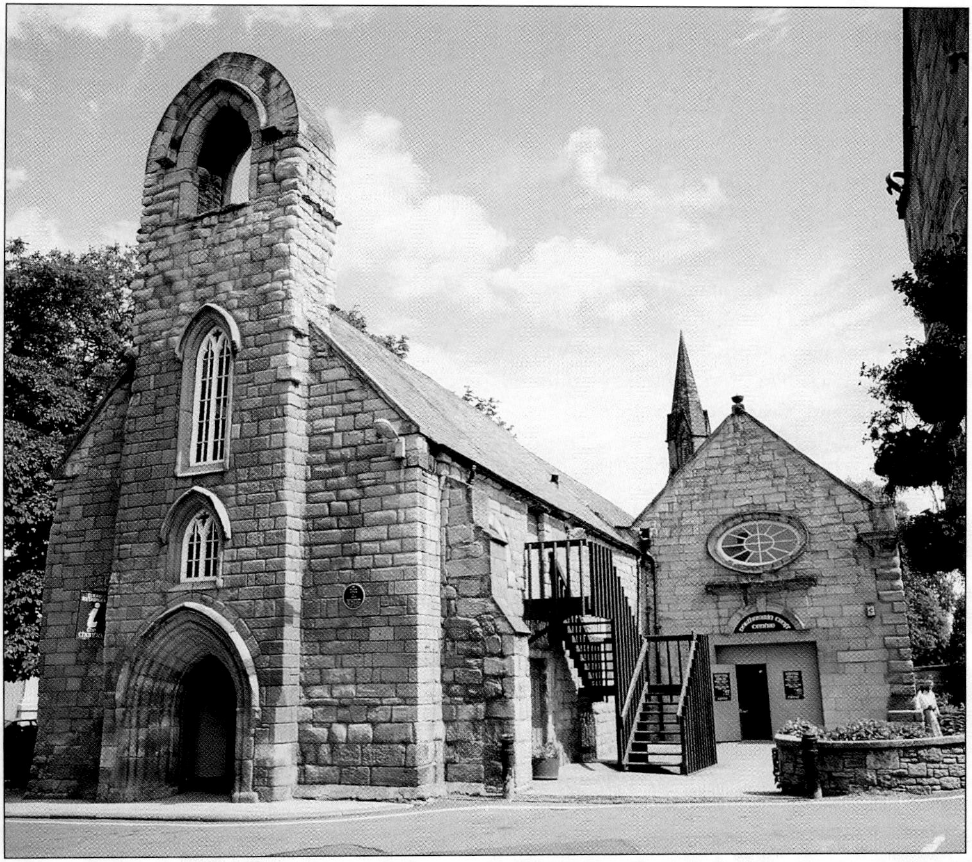

Route description

Start at the bridge in Felton. Take the B6345 uphill (pub on left) towards A1 in direction of Newcastle. At top of hill TL, SP East Thirston/Warkworth Castle/Amble Marina.

1 Cross railway (Railway Inn on RHS).

2 Continue through Acklington.

3 TL onto B6345, SP Amble/Warkworth/ Alnwick/Amble Marina. ***9km (5.5 miles)***

4 TR onto minor road just after Togston Terrace (SP Broomhill back the way).

5 TR at TJ onto A1068, SP Hadston (11km/ 7 miles). Continue and TL after SP Reduce Speed Now on corner.

6 TR at TJ (sea in front of you). The surface here is not all tarmac. Continue as road curves right and pass yellow gate.

7 TL through small wooden gate to continue on track. Follow SP Car Park and then SP Visitor Centre.

8 Rejoin tarmac and go through metal gate (before track turns inland). Continue through wooden gate at left of track and push bike short way along footpath to Druridge Links Nature Reserve car park. Continue to follow road to Cresswell.

9 TR, SP Ellington, and continue into Ellington.

10 TR at TJ, past library.

11 TR at roundabout onto A1068, SP Alnwick.

12 TL, SP Ulgham/Linton. ***22.5km (14 miles)***

13 Cross ford via footpath and bridge.

14 TL at TJ (25.5/16 miles) onto B1337 for climb into Ulgham. Continue through Ulgham and Longhirst to Morpeth.

15 Arrive Morpeth (34.5km/21.5 miles). SO at first roundabout. TR at second roundabout, SP Tynemouth/Newcastle/Alnwick. SO at third roundabout (beside Tourist Information Centre) and continue into town centre (clock tower at far end of main street).

If returning to Morpeth Station, TL at third roundabout (beside Tourist Information Centre) and retrace route to station.

16 Follow main street as it turns up hill to right, heading north.

17 TR onto small road, SP Fulbeck/7.5T except for access (as leave town). Go over stream, keep left and continue up lane.

18 TL at TJ, SP Hebron. Continue into Hebron.

19 TR, SP Cockle Park/Tritlington.

20 TL at TJ, SP Tritlington/Longhorsley. ***42.5km (26.5 miles)***

21 TR, SP Earsdon/Chevington.

22 TR, SP Chevington.

23 TR at TJ, SP Chevington Moor.

24 TL at XR, SP Acklington/Felton/ Eshott/ West Chevington/Amble. ***48km (30 miles)***

25 TL at TJ onto B6345 and return to Felton to complete the ride. ***54.5km (34 miles)***

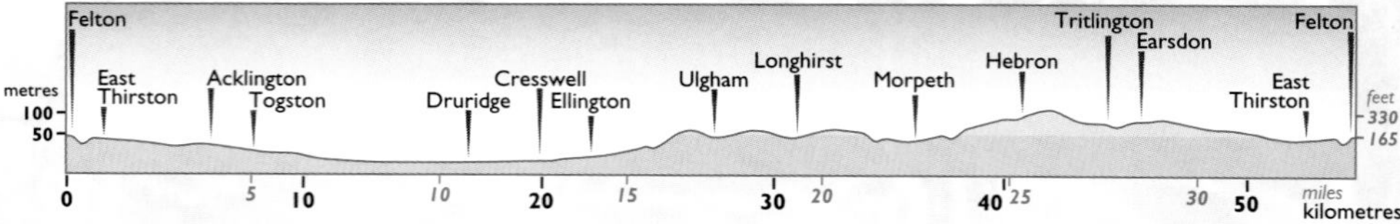

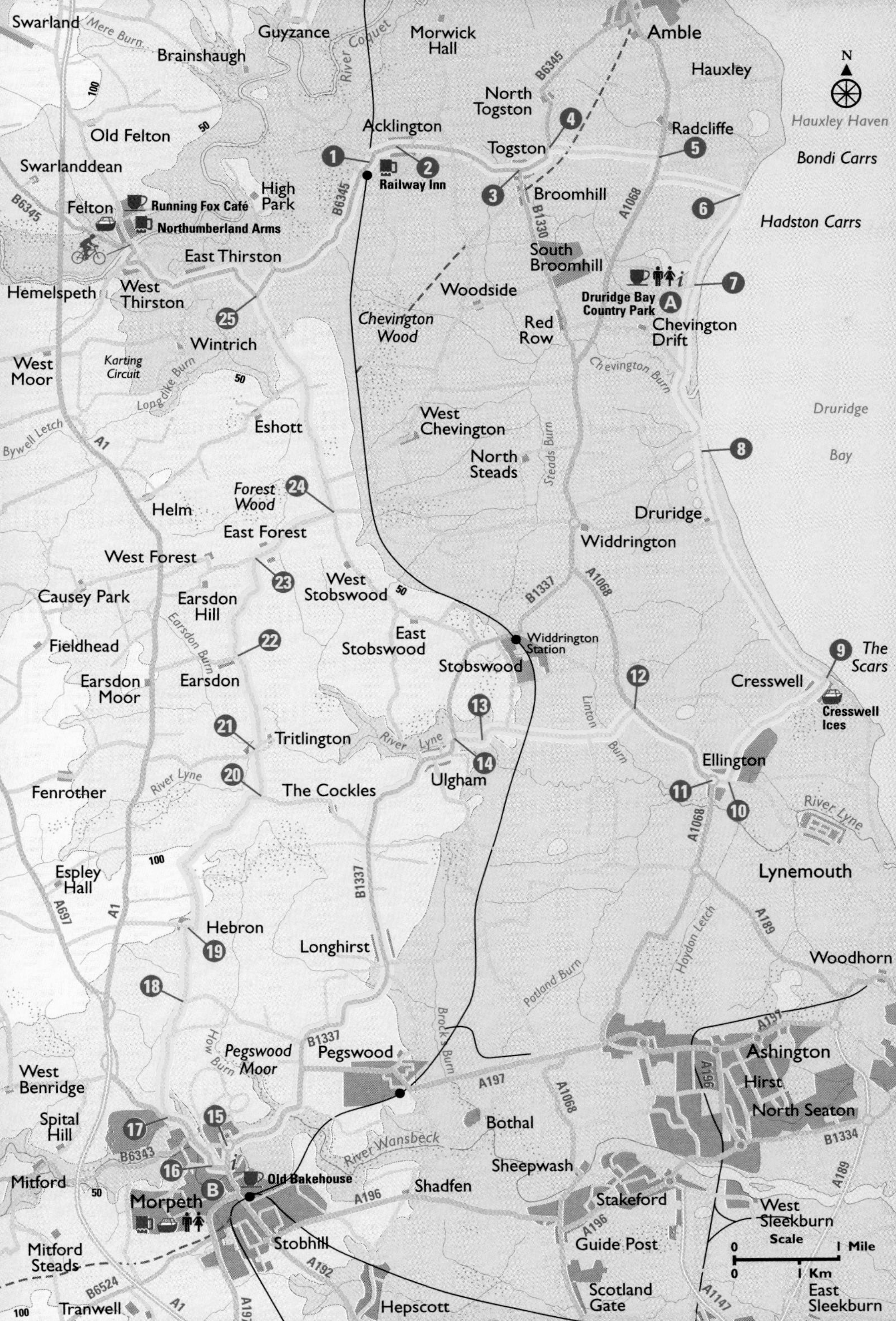

Swarland
Mere Burn
Guyzance
River Coquet
Morwick Hall
Amble
Brainshaugh
Hauxley
North Togston
Old Felton
Acklington
Radcliffe
Hauxley Haven
Togston
Bondi Carrs
Swarlanddean
Railway Inn
Broomhill
Felton
Running Fox Café
High Park
Northumberland Arms
Hadston Carrs
South Broomhill
East Thirston
Hemelspeth
West Thirston
Woodside
Druridge Bay Country Park
Chevington Wood
Red Row
Chevington Drift
Wintrich
West Moor
Karting Circuit
Chevington Burn
Longdike Burn
Druridge
West Chevington
Eshott
Bywell Letch
North Steads
Steads Burn
Bay
Forest Wood
Helm
Druridge
East Forest
Widdrington
West Forest
Causey Park
West Stobswood
Earsdon Hill
Earsdon Burn
East Stobswood
Widdrington Station
Fieldhead
Stobswood
The Scars
Cresswell
Earsdon Moor
Earsdon
Linton Burn
Cresswell Ices
Tritlington
River Lyne
Ellington
Fenrother
The Cockles
Ulgham
River Lyne
Lynemouth
Espley Hall
Hebron
Haydon Letch
Longhirst
Woodhorn
Potland Burn
Brock's Burn
Pegswood Moor
Pegswood
How Burn
Ashington
West Benridge
Hirst
Spital Hill
Bothal
North Seaton
River Wansbeck
Sheepwash
Mitford
Old Bakehouse
Shadfen
Morpeth
Stakeford
West Sleekburn
Guide Post
Stobhill
Mitford Steads
Scale
0
1 Mile
1 Km
Scotland Gate
East Sleekburn
Tranwell
Hepscott
N

Route **14**

CHATTON AND HOLY ISLAND

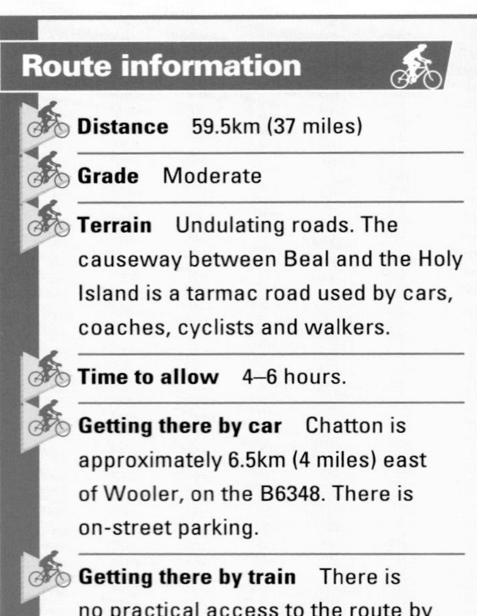

Route information

Distance 59.5km (37 miles)

Grade Moderate

Terrain Undulating roads. The causeway between Beal and the Holy Island is a tarmac road used by cars, coaches, cyclists and walkers.

Time to allow 4–6 hours.

Getting there by car Chatton is approximately 6.5km (4 miles) east of Wooler, on the B6348. There is on-street parking.

Getting there by train There is no practical access to the route by rail.

A spectacular route – north from picturesque Chatton, following the Devil's Causeway over Doddington Moor to Lowick. The route then heads east, crossing the A1 to the Holy Island. Then south, returning through Belford, with fabulous views of the coast and the Cheviot Hills. Note: Holy Island is only accessible when the causeway is open at low tides. Safe crossing times are posted at the start of the causeway and published in the local press, or telephone Berwick-upon-Tweed Tourist Information Centre for crossing times on (01289) 330733.

Places of interest along the route

A Holy Island

The island was known as Lindisfarne until Benedictine Monks settled here in the 11th century. **Lindisfarne Priory** was founded by St Aiden in the 7th century, to convert pagan Northumberland to Christianity. Today visitors can see the impressive ruins of the 11th-century Benedictine monastery (English Heritage). Also exhibition in the visitor centre. Open daily, April to September 1000–1800; October 1000–1700; November to March 1000–1600. Charge. Telephone (01289) 389200. St Cuthbert followed St Aiden to Lindisfarne. A cross marks the site of his chapel, accessible at low tide. **Lindisfarne Castle** (National Trust), originally constructed by the Tudors as protection against Scottish invasion, was restored in the early 20th century by Edward Lutyens. Opening times vary, dependent on low tide. Telephone (01289) 389244.

Route description

Leave Chatton heading west on the B6348 towards Wooler.

1 TR, SP Fowberry. Continue to TJ and TR, SP West Lynham/Belford. Cross River Till via Fowberry Bridge.

2 TL, SP East Horton/West Horton. Continue through Horton into Lowick, along the Devil's

Lindisfarne Castle

Food and drink

There are refreshments available all year on Holy Island, at hotels, pubs and cafes, although the choice is more limited in winter. Belford has a coffee shop (closed Monday) and several pubs offering bar snacks and meals.

Percy Arms Hotel, Chatton

Open daily at lunchtime and in the evening for bar snacks and restaurant meals.

Post Office, Lowick

Post Office with shop and café. Open daily for hot drinks and simple snacks.

White Swan Inn, Lowick

Bar lunches available.

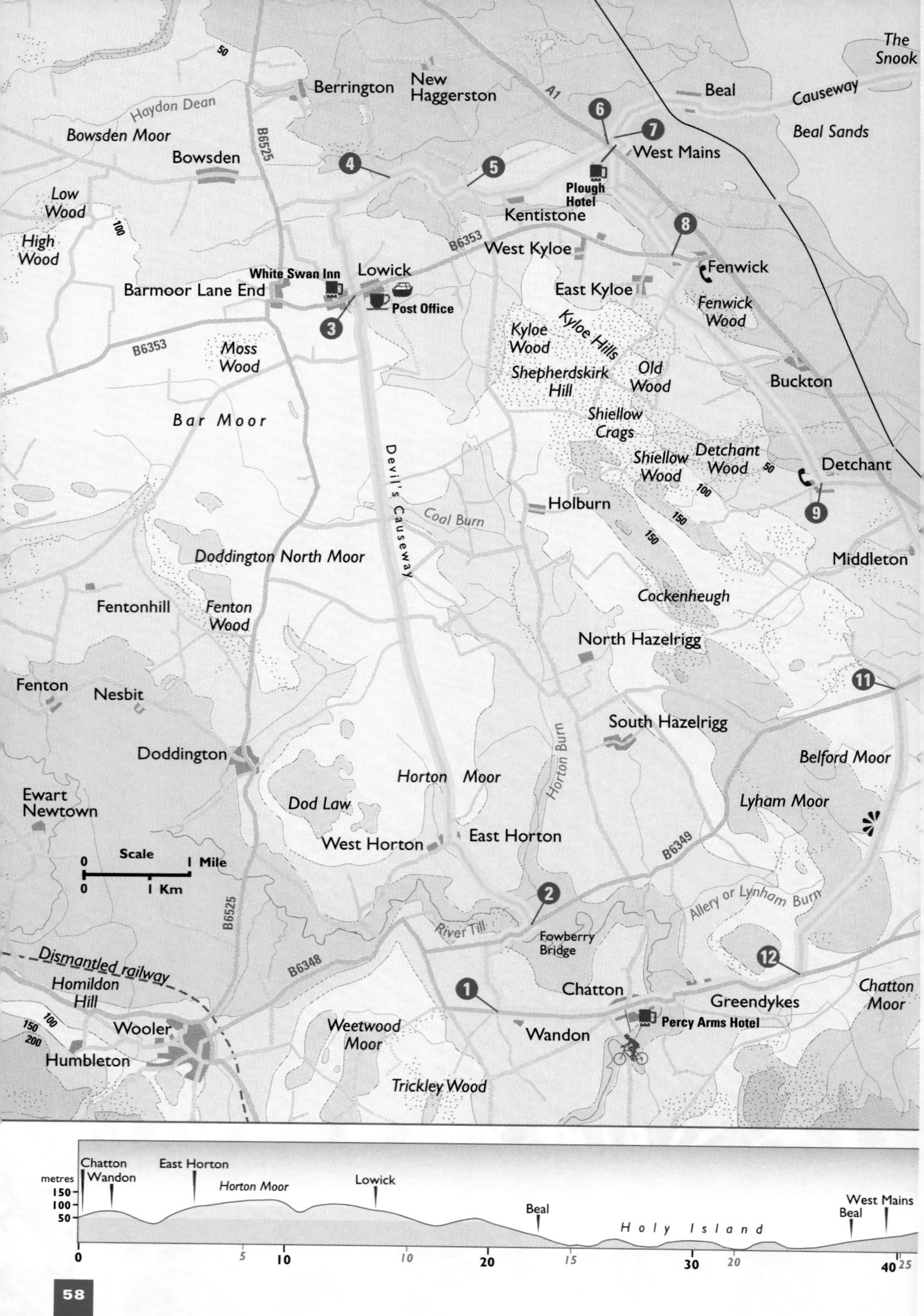

The Snook
Berrington
New Haggerston
Beal
Causeway
Haydon Dean
A1
Beal Sands
Bowsden Moor
B6525
West Mains
Bowsden
Plough Hotel
Low Wood
Kentistone
High Wood
B6353
West Kyloe
White Swan Inn
Lowick
Fenwick
Barmoor Lane End
Post Office
East Kyloe
Fenwick Wood
Kyloe Wood
Kyloe Hills
B6353
Moss Wood
Shepherdskirk Hill
Old Wood
Buckton
Shiellow Crags
Bar Moor
Devil's Causeway
Shiellow Wood
Detchant Wood
Detchant
Coal Burn
Holburn
Doddington North Moor
Middleton
Cockenheugh
Fentonhill
Fenton Wood
North Hazelrigg
Fenton
Nesbit
South Hazelrigg
Horton Burn
Belford Moor
Doddington
Horton Moor
Ewart Newtown
Dod Law
Lyham Moor
East Horton
West Horton
Scale
0 1 Mile
0 1 Km
B6349
B6525
Allery or Lynham Burn
River Till
Fowberry Bridge
Dismantled railway
B6348
Homildon Hill
Chatton
Chatton Moor
Greendykes
Wooler
Weetwood Moor
Wandon
Percy Arms Hotel
Humbleton
Trickley Wood
Chatton
Wandon
East Horton
Horton Moor
Lowick
metres
Beal
Holy Island
West Mains
Beal

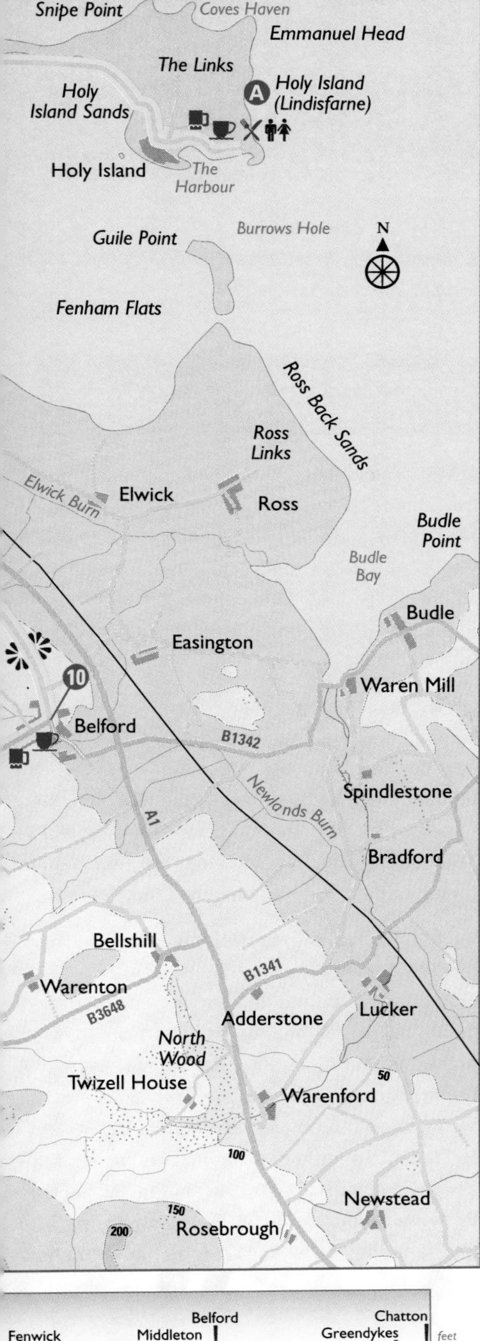

Causeway, a straight Roman road (which can be a hard cycle with a head wind).

3 SO at XR, with White Swan pub opposite, Post Office on RHS (15km/9.5 miles). Continue to TJ, where TR towards coast, no SP.

4 TR at TJ, SP weight limit 33t ahead. Go over bridge and up hill.

5 TR at TJ, SP Lowick/Holborn. Then TL, SP Kentistone/Beal. Continue through Kentistone to XR with A1.

6 SO WITH CARE. Continue over railway crossings, through Beal to causeway. Check tide times so you do not get stranded and continue onto Holy Island (30.5km/19 miles). After visit retrace to junction with A1.

7 TL immediately prior to A1 (in front of Plough Hotel). Continue in front of petrol station. Using cycle path/refuge, cross SO A1 WITH CARE. Follow the little used minor road up and inland.

8 TL at TJ, into Fenwick (41.5km/26 miles). TR to pass in front of telephone box and out of village. Continue into hamlet of Detchant.

9 TL at TJ (by telephone box). Continue, TR at TJ and follow old A1 into Belford.

10 TR onto B6349, SP Wooler.

50.5km (31.5 miles)

11 TL, SP B6348/Wooler/Chatton. Follow this road over Belford Moor (views of Cheviots on RHS) for climb then exhilarating descent to TJ.

12 TR at TJ, SP Chatton/Wooler. Continue descent to Chatton to complete the ride.

59.5km (37 miles)

Route **15**

DERWENT VALLEY RAILWAY PATH – ROWLANDS GILL TO WASKERLEY

Route information

Distance 59.5km (37 miles)

Grade Moderate

Terrain Quiet roads and disused railway tracks. There are some challenging and steep climbs and descents in the second part of the route.

Time to allow 5–7 hours.

Getting there by car Rowlands Gill is south east of Gateshead, at the junction of the A694 and the B6314. There is car parking at the start of the Rowlands Gill/Consett section of the Derwent Valley Railway Path, near the bridge over the River Derwent.

Getting there by train There is no practical rail access to this ride.

From Rowlands Gill the route follows the Derwent Valley Railway Path (DVRP), over spectacular viaducts, to Consett. On across the former site of the steel works, and along the route of the disused Stanhope and Tyne Railway, the Waskerley Way. Then across the Hownsgill Viaduct onto Waskerley Moors, with views of Derwent Reservoir. The final part of the route follows quiet roads, through Edmundbyers, Whittonstall and Chopwell, for a long descent to Rowlands Gill.

Places of interest along the route

A Rowlands Gill

Rowlands Gill is a former Victorian suburb of Newcastle, now a thriving community with a few shops, bank, pub and café. **Gibside** is a 18th-century landscaped park with walks and fine views of the River Derwent. See route 4 for further details.

B Derwent Valley Railway Path

The railway opened in 1867 and at its peak carried half-a-million passengers as well as timber, bricks, coal and iron ore between Newcastle and Consett. The line was closed in 1962 and subsequently converted into a path for leisure use. See route 4 for further details.

C Stanhope and Tyne Railway – the Waskerley Way

This was the route of the earliest public railway on Tyneside, engineered by Robert Stephenson and constructed in 1834. The railway was built to carry limestone and iron ore to the Tyne and also served the Consett steelworks. Now transformed into a path, the line crosses the magnificent **Hownsgill Viaduct**, designed by Thomas Bouch and built in 1858. The viaduct is 213m (700 feet) long and 53m (175 feet) high, spanning a ravine where the River Derwent once flowed.

Gibside

Route description

Start from DVRP car park and cross viaduct onto DVRP.

1 SO through old Ebchester railway station (8km/5 miles). Continue SO.

2 Track changes to tarmac surface. Continue SO over several XRs and across former site of Consett steel works, following DVRP SP Lydgetts Junction.

3 TR onto Waskerley Way (14.5km/9 miles) and across Hownsgill Viaduct. Continue SO across former site of Waskerley Station and picnic area.

Food and drink

There is a pub and several cafés in Rowlands Gill. Consett is a busy town with pubs and cafés on the main street. There is also a tearoom and pub in Edmunbyers and pubs at Ebchester Old Station, Whittonstall and near Chopwell.

Bee Cottage, Waskerley

Popular with C2C cyclists, signposted from the track.

Riding Mill
Beauclerc
Bywell
B6309
Mickley Square
Prudhoe
Frenches Close
Durham Riding
Broomhaugh
Stocksfield
High Mickley
Coalburn
Stanley Burn
Broomley
Painshawfield
Three Horse Shoes
Leadgate
New Ridley
March Burn
A68
Hedley on the Hill
Healey
Apperley
Ravenside
B6309
Chopwell
Stocksfield Burn
Whittonstall
Anchor Inn
Scales Cross
Dere Street Roman road
Hamsterley
Derwent Walk Inn
Minsteracres
Highfield
Newlands
Ebchester
Kiln Pit Hill
Barleyhill
A694
B6310
Shotleyfield
Derwent Reservoir
Birkenside
B6278
Shotley Bridge
B6308
B6309
A691
Black Hedley
Carterway Heads
Greenhead
Consett
B6306
Ruffside
Berry Bank
River Derwent
A692
Edmundbyers
Allensford
Ruffside Moor
Edmundbyers Common
Muggleswick
Castleside
Knitsley
Stanhope & Tyne Railway
Healeyfield
Rowley
Cross Rigg
B6278
Waskerley Way
Hisehope Burn
Moorcock Inn
Chiney
Red House
Muggleswick Common
Black Hill
Hisehope Reservoir
Smiddy Shaw Reservoir
Rippon Burn
Bee Cottage
Butsfield
Horseshoe Hill
Skaylock Hill
Waskerley
Waskerley Beck
Waskerley Reservoir
Scale
0
1 Mile
0
1 Km
Waskerley Park
Collier Law
Tunstall Burn
metres
Rowland's Gill
Lintzford
Consett

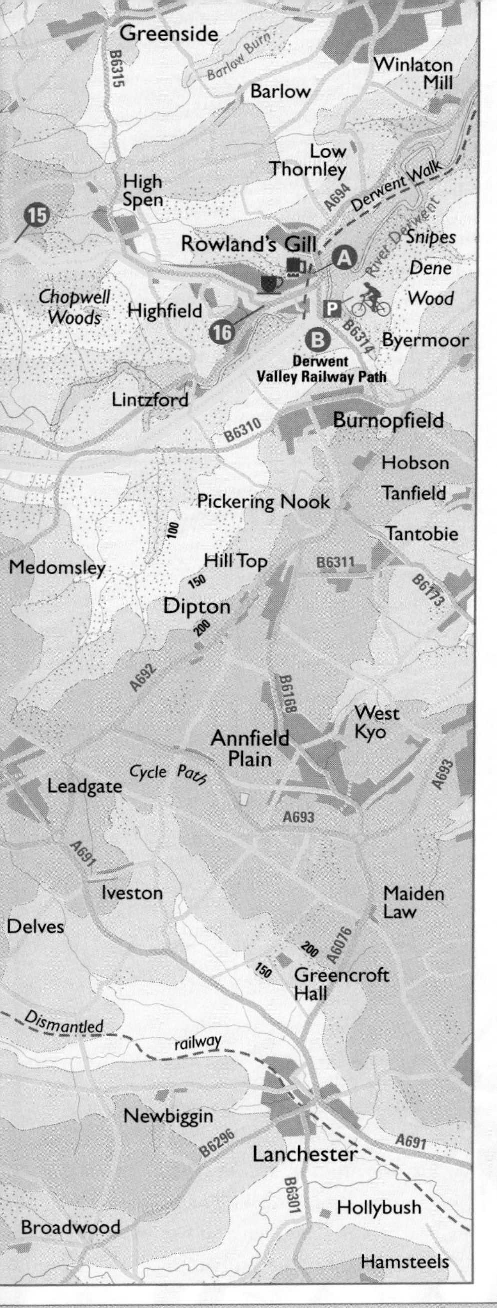

4 TR through picnic area (23km/14.5 miles), then TR at TJ onto road, SP Castleside. Pass Moorcock Inn. TL at TJ and continue into Muggleswick.

5 SO, SP Edmundbyers. Then TL, SP Edmundbyers. TR at TJ into Edmundbyers.

6 Leave Edmundbyers on B6278, SP Shotley Bridge (34.5km/21.5 miles).

7 SO at staggered XR, SP Shotley Bridge, crossing A68 WITH CARE.

8 TL at Snods Edge XR, SP Shotleyfield. Continue and TL at TJ, SP Shotleyfield.

9 TR at TJ, SP Kiln Pit Hill, through Shotley-field.

10 TR at XR, SP Whittonstall. SO at XR, SP Whittonstall and continue SO into Whittonstall.

11 SO staggered XR (46.5km/29 miles), past telephone box and down track. At foot of track, TR SP Bridleway Hollings. LHF at Y junction, up hill past old drift mine entrance. Follow bridleway through farm to TJ with road.

12 TL at TJ onto road. Continue uphill and TR at TJ.

13 TR at TJ. Pass Three Horse Shoes pub. TR at TJ, SP Chopwell, and continue into Chopwell.

14 TL, SP High Spen. TR onto track into woods (just past track to farm/opposite SP Footpath to Leadgate.

15 Continue SO through Chopwell Woods. TL at first TJ. TR at second TJ. Continue SO through Highfield to Rowlands Gill.

16 TL at TJ. Then take second TR, past Post Office and return to car park to complete the ride. ***59.5km (37 miles)***

Waskerley · Edmundbyers · Carterway Heads · Shotleyfield · Highfield · Whittonstall · Ravenside · Leadgate · Rowland's Gill

feet: 980 · 655 · 490 · 330 · 165

miles: 10 · 15 · 20 · 25 · 30 · 35

kilometres: 20 · 30 · 40 · 50

Route **16**

THE TEES VALLEY – SEDGEFIELD TO YARM

Route information

Distance 62.5km (39 miles)

Grade Easy

Terrain Well-surfaced, gently undulating roads.

Time to allow 4–5 hours.

Getting there by car Neasham is south east of Darlington. Take the A167 from Darlington to Croft-on-Tees. Continue through Hurworth-on-Tees to Neasham. Park on the main street in the village.

Getting there by train There are two stations giving access to the route: Dinsdale (see start of route) and Allens West (TR out of station and continue to direction 10). Telephone (0345) 484950 for travel information.

This route covers the southern part of County Durham, dipping into Cleveland and North Yorkshire as it crosses the Tees. The route passes the Stockton to Darlington railway and goes through some charming villages. From Neasham, the route climbs out of the Tees valley, up to Middleton St George, and continues through Great Stainton into Sedgefield. Turning south east to Bishopton, Redmarshall and down to Yarm, before heading west to follow the course of the Tees back to Neasham over the delightful Low Dinsdale Bridge and past the pink sandstone church.

Food and drink

There are many pubs in the villages along the way, usually open county hours (i.e. lunch times and evenings only). Do not rely on obtaining refreshments in these villages, but take advantage of the variety of pubs and cafés in Sedgefield and Yarm.

Number 4, Sedgefield
Tearoom and patisserie. Open all week for light meals, tea and cakes.

Dun Cow, Sedgefield
Bar meals available daily 1200–1345 and from 1900.

Ice Cream Parlour, Yarm
Open all week for light snacks.

Strickland and Holt, Yarm
In the white building beside the clock tower. A good range of light meals, but prices do match its Egon Ronay status. You can keep your bikes safe in the courtyard while you eat.

Near Middleton One Row

Places of interest along the route

Ⓐ Middleton One Row

Much prettier than its parent village, Middleton St George. Middleton One Row comprises one street, built as the railway brought Victorianisation to the area. The Georgian and Victorian buildings look out over the banks of the River Tees to North Yorkshire. The village can be visited at the start of the ride and is seen on the last stretch of the route, on the way to Low Dinsdale Bridge.

Ⓑ Sedgefield

This large village has a wide village green overlooked by an impressive church. The church is open to the public and is well-known for its wood carving, much of which was completed in the 1630s by Robert Barker. The National Hunt racecourse is on the outskirts of the village. **Harwick Hall Country Park**, on the northern side of the town, is a former 18th-century landscaped garden containing the remains of several follies and a serpentine lake. Open daily all year. Admission free.

Ⓒ Yarm

An attractive, thriving market town sited on a loop of the River Tees. The world's first passenger railway, from Stockton on Tees to Darlington, was planned at a meeting in the George and Dragon Inn in 1820. The impressive

metres
100
50
Neasham
Middleton St George
Sadberge
Great Stainton
0
5
10
10
Mainsforth
Bishop Middleham
Sedgefield
Number 4
Dun Cow
Chilton
Rushyford
Bradbury
Woodham
Mordon
Preston Carrs
Newton Aycliffe
Aycliffe Village
Brierley Wood
Wynyard Park
Thorpe Larches
Shotton
Wolviston
Foxton
Elstob
Stillington
Billingham
Thorpe Thewles
Whitton
Norton
Great Stainton
Bishopton
Carlton
Redmarshall
Brafferton
Coatham Mundeville
Newton Kelton
Little Stainton
STOCKTON-ON-TEES
Barmpton
West Newbiggin
East Newbiggin
Hartburn
Great Burdon
Sadberge
Elton
Haughton-le-Skerne
Longnewton
Thornaby-on-Tees
Carter Moor
Burn Wood
Urlay Nook
DARLINGTON
Eaglescliffe
Allens West Station
Dinsdale Station
Oak Tree
Eastbourne
Middleton St George
Teeside International Airport
Ingleby Barwick
Blackwell
Strickland & Holt
Ice Cream Parlour
Yarm
Middleton One Row
High Leven
Low Dinsdale
Hurworth-on-Tees
Croft-on-Tees
Neasham
Low Hail
Black Wood
Moor Plantation
Low Worsall
Pettals Wood
Eryholme
High Worsall
Kirklevington
Girsby
North Wood
Stranbrough Plantation
Dalton on Tees
Low Worsall Moor
Sockburn
Picton
Crathorne
High Worsall Moor
Low Entercommon
Beverley Wood
High Entercommon
Hornby
Scale
0
1 Mile
0
1 Km
Roman Road
River Skerne
Woodham Burn
Shotton Beck
Billingham Beck
Bishopton Beck
Coatham Beck
Cree Beck
River Tees
River Leven
A1(M)
A167
A689
A177
A19
A1027
A139
A1305
A66
A617
A1150
A67
A135
A1044
B1264
B1263
B1265
B1274

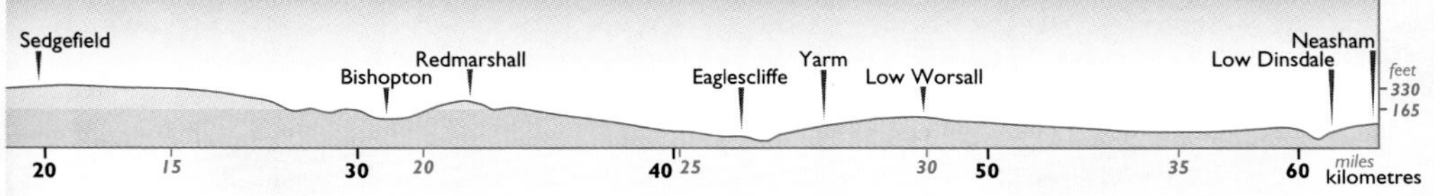

43-arch pink sandstone viaduct, built in the middle of the last century, dominates the town. An interesting footpath, SP Stockton Historic Railway Trail, is signed from the clock tower. Blue information plaques give details of all the significant buildings along the broad, cobbled main street.

Route description

Start from Neasham, heading east. Follow road out of Neasham. TL at XR, up hill, SP Middleton St George (by rotund bus shelter). Continue on this road, passing over Dinsdale Station and SP for Middleton Row.

1 TL at TJ (post office on left) onto old A67. Take first TR (beside Fighting Cocks pub), onto minor road SP Sadberge/Darlington. Continue SO at roundabout, SP Sadberge. Continue into Sadberge.

2 SO at XR, SP Sedgefield.

3 TR at TJ (9.5km/6 miles) onto more major road.

4 To visit Sedgefield continue SO. TR over railway (16.5km/10.5 miles), SP Sedgefield. Continue as road climbs gently past race course. TR at TJ, SP Sedgefield, and continue into village where TR on High Street (by green) for church, shops and pubs. After visit, retrace route.

Otherwise, to continue route TR, SP Bishopton/Stillington.

5 SO at XR.

6 TL at TJ into Bishopton (30.5km/19 miles). Cycle through village, past Talbot pub, church and Blue Bell pub. Follow road round to left, SP Redmarshall. Continue into Redmarshall.

7 TR at XR, into Drovers Lane.

8 TL at TJ, then immediately TR, SP Yarm (CARE, busy junction).

9 SO at two roundabouts, SP Eaglescliffe, and go over A66. Pass Allens West station. Continue.

10 TL at Y junction onto main road.

11 TR at traffic lights into Yarm WITH CARE as there are often traffic queues (42.5km/26.5 miles). Cross river and keep left along cobbled street.

12 Continue through Yarm (clock tower on LHS). TR (where road forks by church), into Walsall Road, and go under viaduct (CARE, often traffic queues).

13 TR at TJ onto B1264, SP Richmond. Continue on B1264 for further 8km (5 miles).

14 TR, SP Girsby/Over Dinsdale/Low Dinsdale.

15 Continue on this road alongside River Tees (views of Middleton One Row).

16 Cross river via single track bridge at Low Dinsdale, pass church on LHS and continue SO into Neasham to finish the ride.

62.5km (39 miles)

Route 17

BELLINGHAM AND KIELDER RESERVOIR

Route information

Distance 62.5km (39 miles)

Grade Strenuous

Terrain Quiet roads and some steep, short hills and gravel tracks.

Time to allow 5 hours.

Getting there by car Bellingham is between Hexham and Otterburn, on the B6320. There is free car parking in the market square and main street, adjacent to the shops and Tourist Information Centre.

Getting there by train There is no practical railway access to the route.

From Bellingham following a section of the Reivers Way, a cycle route running between Tynemouth and Whitehaven, via Kielder and Carlisle. The route follows quiet roads along the south side of Kielder Reservoir and on to challenging tracks in Kielder Forest. The route returns to Bellingham along the pleasant, gated road through Falstone. Visitors are well catered for in summer – in winter you should carry food and drinks with you.

Places of interest along the route

A Bellingham

An attractive market town on the River North Tyne, on the edge of Northumberland National Park. The town has several churches, notably **St Cuthbert's** on the west side of the market square. The church is said to be on the site of one of the resting places of the monks who carried Saint Cuthbert's coffin when forced to flee from Lindesfarne. Cannon balls were found in the roof during restoration work, said to be from Cromwell's army as they tried to forge the river. The church is open to visitors. The **Heritage Centre** describes the history of the North Tyne Valley through photographs and maps. Open May to September, Friday–Monday 1330–1630; Easter and Bank Holiday Mondays 1130–1630. Charge. Telephone (01434) 220050. Also in Bellingham, **Black Middens Bastle House** (English Heritage) is a 16th-century stone built farmhouse. Access at all reasonable times. **Harshaw Dene** is an attractive woodland walk to a waterfall. Access at all reasonable times.

B Kielder Reservoir and Kielder Forest

Northern Europe's largest man-made lake, with 43km (27 miles) of shoreline and a surface area of 1,086ha (2,684 acres), set in Europe's largest man-made forest. The lake, surrounded by superb scenery, was opened in 1982, and caters for the outdoor enthusiast (cycle hire, cycling and walking tracks and a wide range of water based activity). The upper part of the reservoir is a conservation area, with numerous species of birds and other wildlife and super views. Kielder Forest comprises four forests – Kielder, Falstone, Wark and Redesdale, established between 1940 and 1970. There are three visitor centres along the lake. **Leapish Waterside Park** (swimming pool, birds of prey, restaurant) is open daily, April to October 1000–1600; May to September 1000–1700. Telephone (01434) 250312. **Tower Knowle Visitor Centre** (tourist information, boat trips, restaurant) is open daily, April and October

1000–1600; May to September 1000–1700; November to March 1000–1600. Telephone (01434) 240398. **Kielder Castle Forest Park Centre** (forest shop, exhibitions, tearoom) is open April to October, daily 1000–1700 (August closes 1800); November and December, weekends 1100– 1600. Telephone (01434) 250209.

Ⓒ Falstone

A charming village on the quieter, north side of the reservoir, predating the Norman Conquest. Within Falstone parish, 45 homes were flooded as part of the construction of Kielder Reservoir. The tearoom houses a National Park Information Point. Open March to September, daily 09001800; October to February, Friday–Sunday, 0900–1600. Telephone (01434) 240261.

Food and drink

Bellingham has pubs, a tearoom and a shop. During the summer, there is plenty of choice along Kielder Reservoir at the visitor centres.

Fountain Café, Bellingham

Situated in the Tourist Information Centre, serving light snacks and hot drinks.

Rose and Crown, Bellingham

In the market square, serving bar meals.

Falstone Tearoom, Falstone

Tearoom and craft shop.

Route description

Start at the Tourist Information Centre in Bellingham. Cycle through the town, with the town hall clock on LHS. Pass Black Bull pub on LHS. Take B6320 towards Wark (ignoring TR on corner, SP Kielder). Cross bridge.

1 TR (after bridge), SP Reivers/Unsuitable for Heavy Vehicles.

2 TL at TJ, SP Stannersburn/Falstone/ Kielder/Newcastleton (8km/5 miles). Continue towards reservoir.

3 Pass picnic site and public toilet at Hawkhope and Towerknowe. ***16km (10 miles)***

4 Pass Leaplish Waterside Park on RHS (22.5km/14 miles). Continue.

5 TR, SP Community Centre/Village Shop/ Bryness/Kielder Castle/Forest Park Centre.

6 To visit Kielder Castle visitor centre, TL over bridge and past Anglers Arms (at top of hill there is a Richard Cainke sculpture). Otherwise, continue SO.

7 Continue past forestry cottages to speed limit SP. TL uphill, SP Gowanburn access/ Kielder Dam/Falstone. ***31.5km (19.5 miles)***

8 Take LHF onto gravel track, SP No Motor Vehicles. Continue.

9 Pass picnic site and commemorative plaque. ***42.5km (26.5 miles)***

10 Take RHF (not gravelled), SP No Lorry Access.

11 TR at TJ and descend to TJ by disused railway bridge.

12 To visit Falstone, TR under bridge. Otherwise, TL to continue route (45km/ 28 miles), along gated road to Lanehead.

13 TR at TJ then immediately TL, SP Hexham/Bellingham. ***53km (33 miles)***

14 TL at TJ onto B6320, SP Bellingham (58km/36 miles). Continue into Bellingham to complete the ride. ***62.5km (39 miles)***

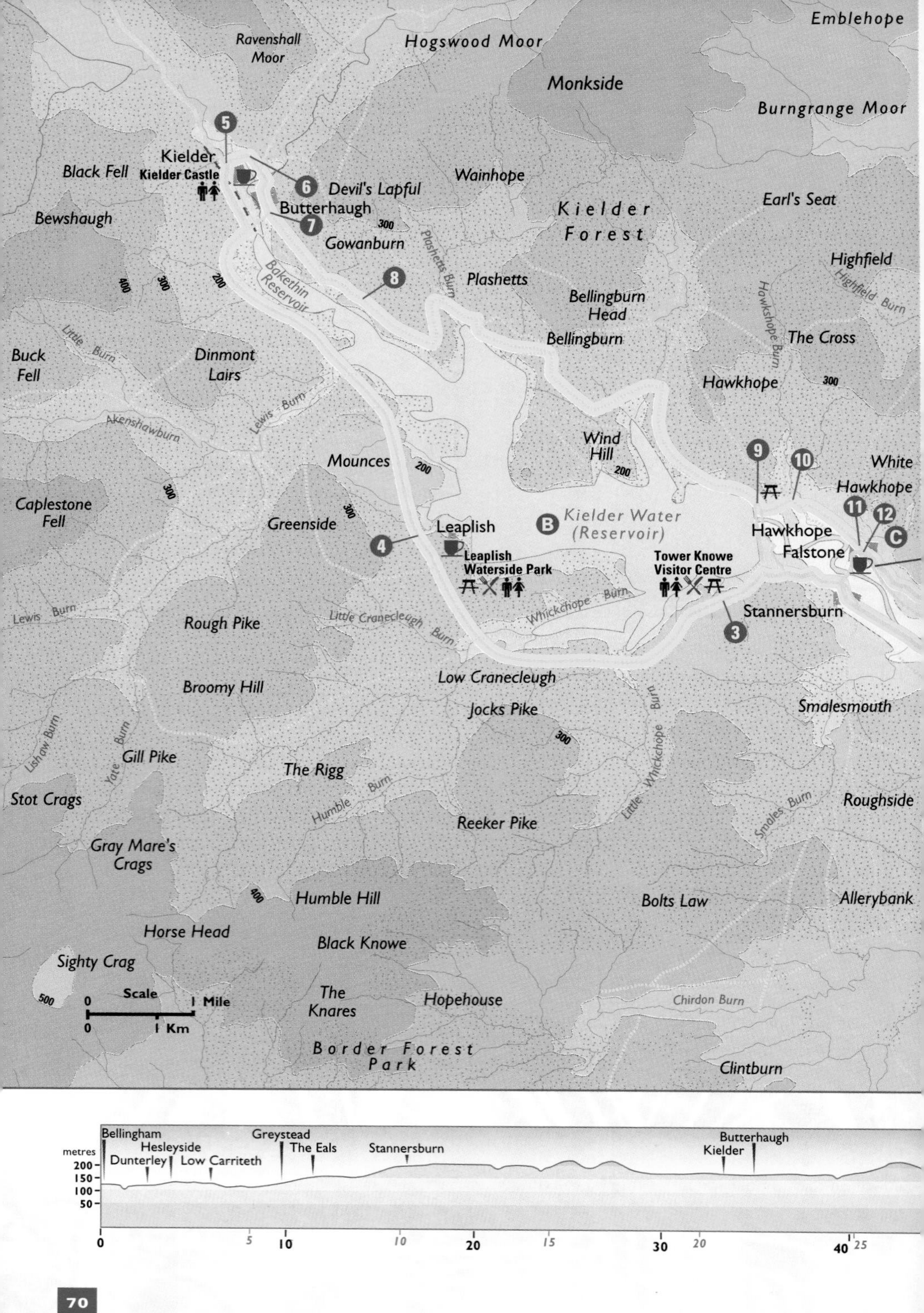
Emblehope
Ravenshall Moor
Hogswood Moor
Monkside
Burngrange Moor
Kielder
Kielder Castle
Black Fell
Devil's Lapful
Wainhope
Butterhaugh
Bewshaugh
Gowanburn
Kielder Forest
Earl's Seat
Highfield
Highfield Burn
Bakethin Reservoir
Plashetts Burn
Plashetts
Bellingburn Head
Hawkshope Burn
The Cross
Bellingburn
Little Burn
Buck Fell
Dinmont Lairs
Hawkhope
Lewis Burn
Akenshawburn
Wind Hill
White Hawkhope
Mounces
Caplestone Fell
Kielder Water (Reservoir)
Greenside
Leaplish
Hawkhope
Falstone
Leaplish Waterside Park
Tower Knowe Visitor Centre
Lewis Burn
Whickhope Burn
Stannersburn
Rough Pike
Little Cranecleugh Burn
Low Cranecleugh
Broomy Hill
Jocks Pike
Smalesmouth
Lishaw Burn
Yate Burn
Gill Pike
Whickhope Burn
The Rigg
Little
Stot Crags
Humble Burn
Smales Burn
Roughside
Reeker Pike
Gray Mare's Crags
Humble Hill
Bolts Law
Allerybank
Horse Head
Black Knowe
Sighty Crag
Scale
0
1 Mile
0
1 Km
The Knares
Hopehouse
Chirdon Burn
Border Forest Park
Clintburn
metres
Bellingham
Hesleyside
Dunterley
Low Carriteth
Greystead
The Eals
Stannersburn
Butterhaugh
Kielder

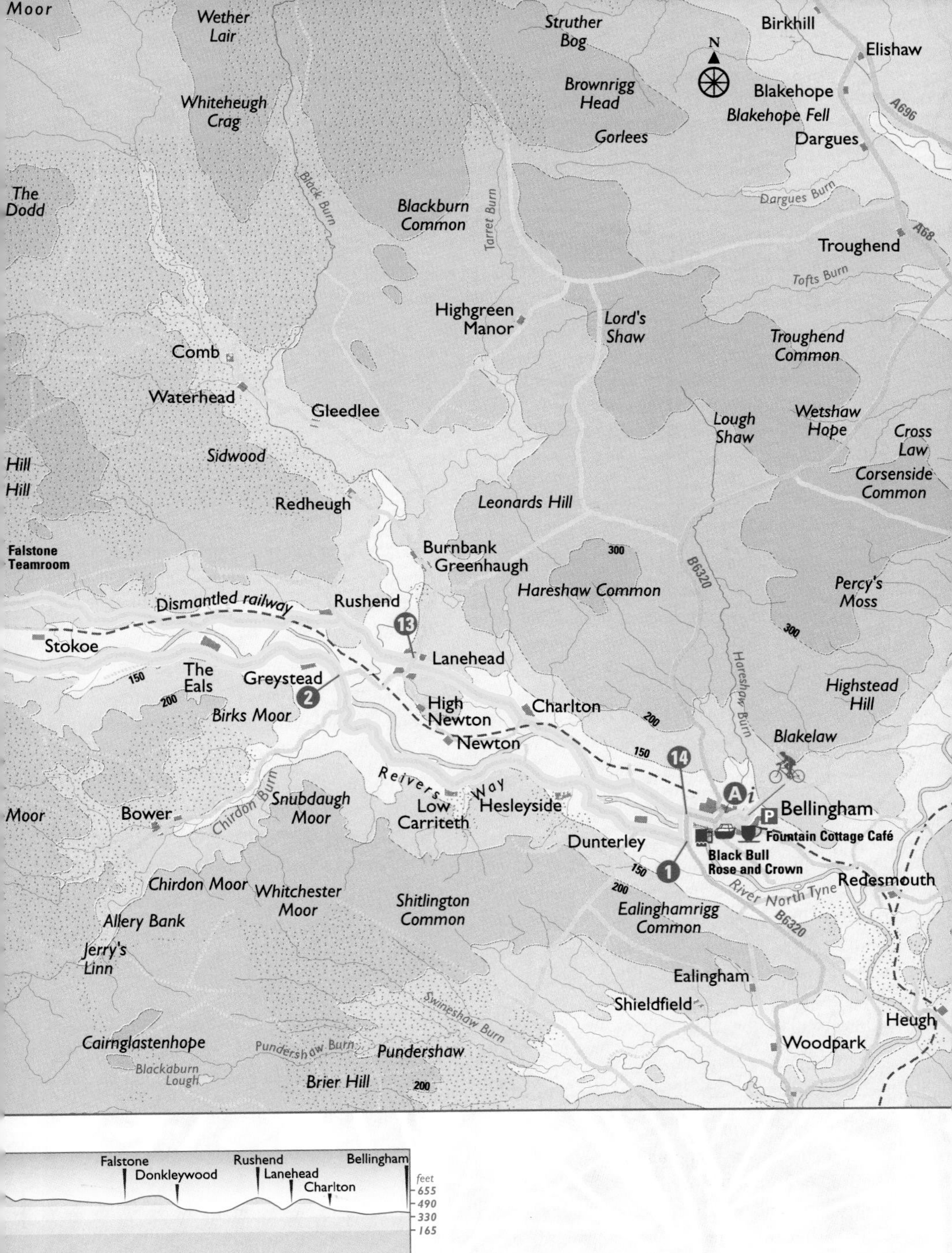

Moor
Wether Lair
Struther Bog
Birkhill
Elishaw
N
Brownrigg Head
Blakehope
Blakehope Fell
A696
Whiteheugh Crag
Gorlees
Dargues
The Dodd
Black Burn
Blackburn Common
Tarret Burn
Dargues Burn
A68
Troughend
Tofts Burn
Highgreen Manor
Lord's Shaw
Troughend Common
Comb
Waterhead
Gleedlee
Lough Shaw
Wetshaw Hope
Cross Law
Sidwood
Hill
Hill
Corsenside Common
Redheugh
Leonards Hill
Falstone Teamroom
Burnbank
Greenhaugh
300
B6320
Hareshaw Common
Percy's Moss
Dismantled railway
Rushend
300
13
Stokoe
Lanehead
Hareshaw Burn
150
The Eals
Greystead
Highstead Hill
200
2
High Newton
Charlton
Birks Moor
200
Newton
Blakelaw
150
14
Reivers Way
Chirdon Burn
A
i
Moor
Bower
Snubdaugh Moor
Low Carriteth
Hesleyside
P
Bellingham
Fountain Cottage Café
Dunterley
Black Bull
Rose and Crown
150
1
Redesmouth
200
River North Tyne
Chirdon Moor
Whitchester Moor
Shitlington Common
Ealinghamrigg Common
B6320
Allery Bank
Jerry's Linn
Ealingham
Shieldfield
Swineshaw Burn
Heugh
Cairnglastenhope
Pundershaw Burn
Pundershaw
Woodpark
Blackaburn Lough
Brier Hill
200
Falstone
Donkleywood
Rushend
Lanehead
Charlton
Bellingham
feet
655
490
330
165
30
35
40
miles
50
60
kilometres

Route **18**

ALLENDALE, ALLENHEADS AND BLANCHLAND

Route information

Distance 63.5km (39.5 miles)

Grade Strenuous

Terrain Climbs and descents, with challenging off-road sections across open moorland. This route is best undertaken on a clear day, during dry weather.

Time to allow 6–8 hours.

Getting there by car Allendale Town is on the B6295 south west of Hexham, off the A686 and the A689. There is car parking in the market place.

Getting there by train There is no practical railway access to the route.

This route climbs from Allendale Town across Hexhamshire Common, down into East Allen Dale to Allendale. Another climb and descent lead from Rookhope Burn to Blanchland in the Derwent valley. The route then follows a track over Bulbeck Common to Slaley Forest, before returning to Allendale.

Places of interest along the route

A Allendale Town

Know as the valley of the shining water and the geographical centre of Britain. Originally a centre for lead mining: the ore was brought down from the fells to be smelted here. The town and surrounding area features in Catherine Cookson's *Mallen Family.* Allendale Fair takes place at the end of May and the agricultural show is held in mid-August. The most famous annual event is the New Years Eve tar barrel ceremony, during which guisers parade through the town in fancy dress, carrying flaming barrels of tar on their heads.

B Allenheads

Founded on lead mining, Allenheads is reputed to be the highest village in England. A Heritage Centre and Blacksmiths Shop are open daily in summer and at various times during winter (telephone to confirm times on 01434 685395). A working Armstrong hydraulic engine is on view opposite the shop. The C2C long distance cycle route goes through the village.

C Blanchland

A charming estate village built around a 12th-century monastery of 1175, hidden deep in a valley. See route 9 for further detail.

Food and drink

Allendale Town has several pubs and a café in the village square (the Golden Lion and the Kings Head are recommended for bar meals).

Hemmel Café, Allenheads

Popular with C2C cyclists. Open daily for light meals. Seating inside and out.

White Monk Tearooms, Blanchland

Open daily in summer only.

Lord Crewe Arms, Blanchland

Teas, coffees and meals available in a fascinating building.

River East Allen, near Allenheads

Route description

Start in the market place, Allendale Town. Take the Shilburn road (heading east), climb past High Strothers Farm. SO at gate, SP Hexhamshire. Continue onto common and SO at next two XR, SP Kingslaw Plantation.

1 TL at gate onto road (over bridge) and SO at XR. ***5.5km (3.5 miles)***

2 TR at second plantation onto track, SP Public Bridleway, for steady climb then descent to XR.

3 SO at XR, past post with white disc. After a short uphill scramble, TL through gate. Continue to TR then SO through another gate. ***12km (7.5 miles)***

4 TR at post with blue arrow, as valley comes into view ahead (18.5km/11.5 miles). Follow posts down to road.

5 TL onto road. Continue through Allenheads.

6 Leave village on road SP Rookhope (C2C). Continue SO over top into County Durham, following Rookhope Burn.

7 TL, SP Blanchland (27km/17 miles). Climb steeply then descend into Townfield.

8 TR, SP C2C (33.5km/21 miles). Then TL, SP Blanchland, staying on C2C.

9 TL at TJ, SP Blanchland. Continue and TR at TJ, SP Derwent Reservoir.

10 TL at TJ (39.5km/24.5 miles), over bridge and into Blanchland. Leave Blanchland on road SP Baybridge. Continue to Baybridge.

11 TR beside cottages and continue up hill on road.

12 TL through gate, SP Birkside Farm. Continue through gate uphill to right. Follow track to left. After a short while track becomes ill defined, but follow it over ridge to right. Continue on track and SO through gate.

13 SO at XR (green hut on LHS).

14 TL (on track) just before reaching Slaley Forest (45.5km/28.5 miles). Follow track down hill, through three gates, into woods. TR to follow track alongside Devil's Water. Either cross stream using ford then recross it via footbridge, or stay on right bank as far as footbridge.

15 Continue up steps, SP Embley, and across field. Follow power lines up hill to gate.

16 Go through gate to farm and continue SO.

17 Take LHF at Y junction, then TR at TJ. Continue to Whitley Chapel.

18 TL at XR, SP Eshells (53km/33 miles). TR at TJ, SP Dalton. TL at XR, SP Eshells. Continue to Eshells Farm.

19 TL at TJ (at farm) on to track. SO through gate, SP Allendale. Follow posts with white discs (parallel to shooting butts with burn on left) as far as TJ.

20 TL at TJ onto road. Then, TL at TJ and continue into Allendale to complete the ride. ***63.5km (39.5 miles)***

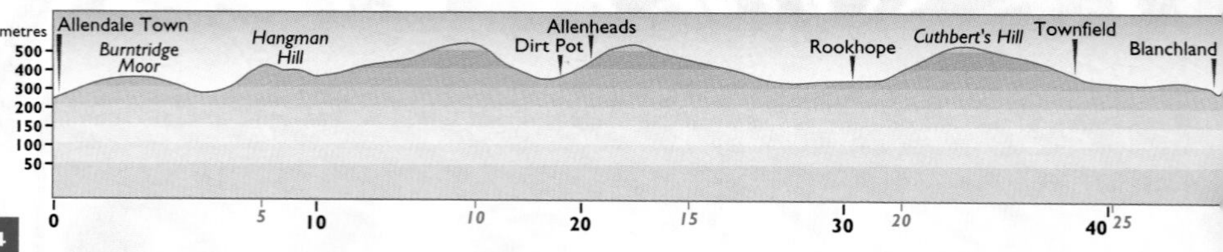

N
Dotland
Ordley
Juniper
Steel
Dipton Wood
Devils Water
Dalton
Whitley Chapel
Dukesfield
Slaley
B6306
Spitalshield Moor
Anchley Sike
Coldcoats Sike
Catton
Lough Hill
Reeds Rigg
Eshells Moor
Eshells Farm
B6295
B6303
Allendale Town
Crawberry Hill
Burntridge Moor
Rowley Burn
Herds Law
Stobb Cross
Hexhamshire Common
Slaley Forest
Embley Fell
Acton Fell
Acton Burn
Potter Burn
East Allen Dale
Studdon
Broad Mere
Linn Burn
Broadwell House
Blanchland Moor
Burntshielhaugh Fell
Cowbyers Fell
Sinderhope
Lilswood Moor
Hangman Hill
Devils Water
Birkside Fell
Allendale Common
Pikeley Rigg
Hope Fell
White Monk Tearooms
Harwoodshield Fell
Bulbeck Common
Baybridge
Blanchland
Lord Crewe Arms
Sipton Shield
Riddlehamhope Fell
Beldon Burn
Tedham Moss
Spartylea
Halleywell
Nookton Back Fell
Hunstanworth
Townfield
River East Allen
Swinhope Burn
Quickcleugh Burn
Heatheryburn Moor
Nookton Fell
Boltshope Park
Nookton Burn
Dikehead Dam
Nookton Edge
Dirt Pot
Quickcleugh Common
Hemmel Café
Allenheads
Allenheads Inn
Black Hags
Cuthbert's Hill
Burnhead Dam
Bolt's Law
Middlehope Moor
Allenheads Park
Corbitmere Dam
Redburn Common
Stanhope Burn
Bell's Hill
South Foul Sik
Rockhope Chimney
Rookhope Burn
Wolfcleugh Common
Puddingthorn Moor
Stanhope Common
Rookhope
Burtree Fell
Middlehope Moor
White Edge
Lintzgarth Common
Snailsburn Common
Rook Hope
Long Hill
Cornriggs
Hangingwells Common
Copthill
Scale
0
1 Mile
0
1 Km
A
B
C
1
2
3
4
5
6
7
8
9
10
11
12
13
14
15
16
17
18
19
20
Baybridge
Blanchland Moor
Whitley Chapel
Allendale Town
Eshells Moor
feet
1630
1305
980
655
490
330
165
30
50
35
60
40
miles
kilometres

Route **19**

BELSAY, CHESTERS ROMAN FORT AND HEXHAM

Route information

Distance 73km (45.5 miles)

Grade Strenuous

Terrain Hilly roads, with a couple of flat off-road sections.

Time to allow 5–7 hours.

Getting there by car Belsay is 22.5km (14 miles) north west of Newcastle on the A696. There is car parking at the Blacksmith's Coffee Shop, at the entrance to Belsay Castle at the southern end of the village.

Getting there by train There is no railway station at Belsay. However, the route may be joined at Hexham, on the Newcastle/Carlisle line, telephone (0345) 484950 for travel information. TR out of the station and join the route at direction 10, where cross bridge over River Tyne.

From Belsay, the route climbs and descends, passing through Wallridge, Ingoe, Ryal and Bingfield. Descending to cross the River North Tyne at Chollerford, the route then climbs and drops again to cross the River Tyne at Warden. A flat off-road section through Hexham is followed by a long hard climb through Acomb and onto Stagshaw. The final section is easier, through rolling hills via Great Whittington, Matfen and Stamfordham, back to Belsay.

Places of interest along the route

A Belsay

Belsay village was built in the 1830s. It has a distinctive arcaded row of brown stone cottages, one housing the shop and post office. **Belsay Hall Castle**, one of the finest English tower houses in the north, is a neo-classical style hall and 13th-century castle set in 12ha (30 acres) of gardens and woodland, including ornate terraces and a quarry garden with sunken croquet lawns. English Heritage property. Open daily, April to September 1000–1800; October 1000–1700; November to March 1000–1600. Charge. Telephone (01661) 881636.

B Chesters Roman Fort and Museum

The best-preserved Roman cavalry fort in Britain with extensive bathhouse remains in a riverside setting. English Heritage property. Café. Open daily, April to September 0930–1800; October 1000–1700; November to March 1000–1600. Charge. Telephone (01434) 681379.

C Hexham

A bustling town dominated by history and popular with visitors keen to explore nearby Hadrian's Wall. See route 9 for further details.

Chesters Roman Fort

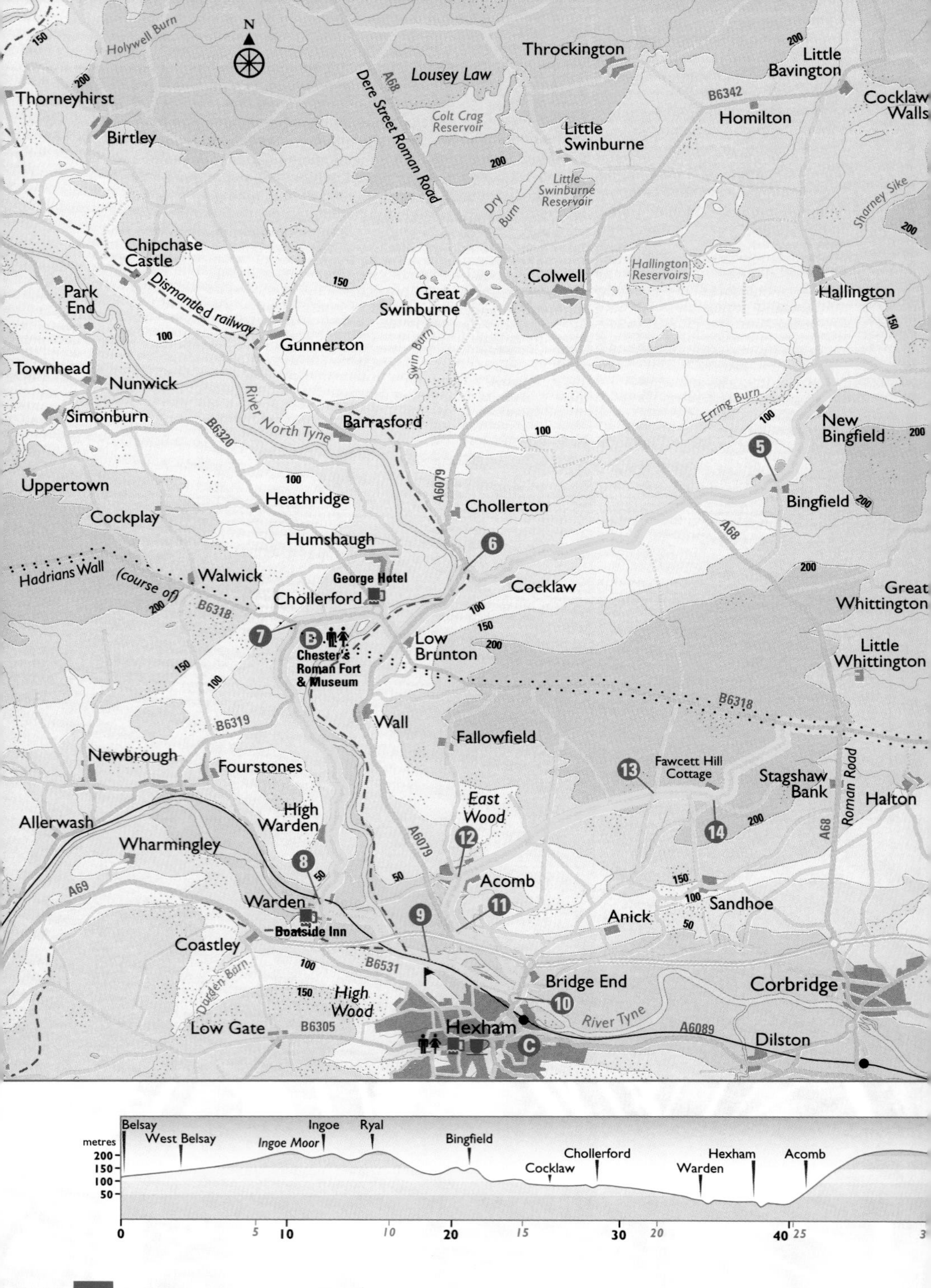
N
Holywell Burn
Thorneyhirst
Birtley
Throckington
Lousey Law
Colt Crag Reservoir
A68
Dere Street Roman Road
Little Bavington
B6342
Homilton
Cocklaw Walls
Little Swinburne
Little Swinburne Reservoir
Dry Burn
Sharney Sike
Chipchase Castle
Dismantled railway
Park End
Great Swinburne
Colwell
Hallington Reservoirs
Hallington
Gunnerton
Swin Burn
Townhead
Nunwick
Simonburn
River North Tyne
B6320
Barrasford
Erring Burn
New Bingfield
Uppertown
Heathridge
A6079
Chollerton
Bingfield
Cockplay
Humshaugh
Hadrians Wall (course of)
Walwick
George Hotel
Chollerford
Cocklaw
Great Whittington
B6318
Chester's Roman Fort & Museum
Low Brunton
Little Whittington
B6319
Wall
Fallowfield
Newbrough
Fourstones
Fawcett Hill Cottage
Stagshaw Bank
Roman Road
Halton
East Wood
High Warden
Allerwash
Wharmingley
Acomb
A69
Warden
Boatside Inn
Anick
Sandhoe
Coastley
B6531
Darden Burn
Bridge End
Corbridge
High Wood
River Tyne
Low Gate
B6305
Hexham
A6089
Dilston
metres
Belsay
West Belsay
Ingoe
Ingoe Moor
Ryal
Bingfield
Cocklaw
Chollerford
Warden
Hexham
Acomb

Sir Edward's Lake
Hillhead
Sandybraes
Bradford
A696
River Blyth
B6524
East Trewick
Hedchester Law
Ogle
Blacksmith's Coffee Shop
Belsay
Ogle Burn
Bankfoot
Belsay Hall Castle
Kirkley March
Tod Hill
Kirkheaton
Coal Burn
Wallridge
B6309
East Newham
Middle Newham
Kearsley Fell
Devil's Causeway Roman Road
Black Heddon
Bygate
Ingoe Moor
West Newham
Westgate
Blackheadon Burn
Milbourne
Higham Dykes
Ingoe
Ryal
Robsheugh
Heugh
Small Burn
Fenwick
Grindstonelaw
Stamfordham
Dalton
River Pont
Matfen
Hawkwell
Medburn
Eachwick
Ouston
Ouston Moor
River Pont
West Moorhouses
B6309
Harlow Hill
East Heddon
Whitchester
Vallum (course of)
B6318
A69
Rudchester
Houghton
B6321
Shildonhill
Bogle Burn
B6309
B6528
Heddon-on-the-Wall
Aydon
Old Nafferton
Horsley
Dismantled railway
Brockhole Burn
River Tyne
Wylam
A69
Scale
0
1 Mile
0
1 Km
Newton
Clara Vale
Bearl
Ovingham
A695
Crawcrook
B6317
Ovington
Prudhoe
Great Whittington
Matfen
Stamfordham
Black Heddon
West Belsay
Belsay
feet
655
490
330
165
50
35
60
40
70
45
miles
kilometres

Route description

Start at the top of the drive to Belsay Castle, at the junction with the A696 Newcastle/Jedburgh road. TL onto A696 (heading north).

1 TL, SP Kirkheaton, for 3km (2 miles), to continue SO at TJ, SP Kirkheaton.

2 TL, SP Wallridge. Continue and TR at XR, SP Ryal (7km/4.5 miles). Go through Wallridge to TJ where TL, SP Ingoe, and descend hill.

3 TR, SP Matfen (Ingoe is on left). Continue and TR at TJ, SP Ryal.

4 SO at XR, SP Reivers, for steep descent. TL at XR, SP Bingfield and go uphill to TR at TJ, no SP.

5 TR at TJ, SP Chollerton. Then SO at staggered XR with A68, SP Chollerton. Continue to TJ with A6079.

6 TL at TJ, no SP (25km/15.5 miles). TR at XR, SP Chollerford. Cross bridge over North Tyne to roundabout (George Hotel on right). TL at roundabout, SP Carlisle. Pass Chesters Roman Fort on left.

7 TL at TJ, SP Haydon Bridge. Then TL at TJ, SP Warden.

8 TL at TJ, SP Hexham (Boatside Inn is on right, 33.5km/21 miles). Cross bridge over Tyne and immediately TL, no SP. Follow this narrow lane under and then alongside railway line – it passes under road bridge and then becomes rough track. Continue.

9 TL at level crossing gate (36km/22.5 miles), to follow track along avenue of trees (golf course RHS, river LHS). Go through park.

10 Have a look around Hexham. Or, to continue route, TL out of park, over bridge across River Tyne. TL (well before big roundabout and just before SP Kielder Water). TL, SP Bridleway to Acomb. Continue on this track, across A69, then TL, SP Bridleway.

11 TR at end of bridleway onto road, no SP (39.5km/24.5 miles). Then, TR, SP Acomb.

12 TR at TJ, no SP, and SO, SP Stagshaw. Keep SO at next two junctions, SP Stagshaw.

13 SO at XR, SP Fawcett Hill. SO at next junction, SP Fawcett Hill.

14 TL at XR, SP Stagshaw (46.5km/29 miles). Continue on gated lane through farm to TJ where TR onto B6318, no SP. Continue to roundabout and SO, SP Newcastle.

15 TL, SP Great Whittington. Continue through village and TR, SP Matfen.

16 TL at TJ, SP Stamfordham (55.5km/34.5 miles). Continue through Matfen, Fenwick and into Stamfordham.

17 Take LHF, SP Belsay. Immediately TL. SO at next junctions, SP Belsay.

18 Follow road round to right, SP Belsay. SO at staggered XR, SP Bolam.

19 TR at TJ, SP Belsay. TL at TJ, SP Newcastle, and finish the route at the top of the drive to Belsay Castle. ***73km (45.5 miles)***

Food and drink

Plenty of choice in Hexham (the Wentworth Café is recommended), a tea-room and pub in Matfen, and pubs in Great Whittington and Stamfordham.

Blacksmiths Coffee Shop, Belsay

At the start and end of the ride and open daily. Home-cooking in pleasant surroundings.

George Hotel, Chollerford

A well-known establishment serving a high standard of drinks, bar and restaurant meals.

Boatside Inn, Warden

Nice country pub serving bar meals.

Route **20**

WOOLER, KIRK YETHOLM AND BRANXTON

Route information

Distance 74km (46 miles)

Grade Moderate

Terrain On-road. There are several stiff climbs after Branxton and low gears are required.

Time to allow 5–7 hours.

Getting there by car Wooler is on the A697, south of Coldstream. Park at the pay and display car park opposite the Tourist Information Centre.

Getting there by train There is no practical railway access to the route.

From Wooler the route heads west, following the River Glen and the Bowmont Water across the border to Kirk Yetholm. The route then turns north to Branxton, and then east across Ford Common, with views of the east coast and the Cheviot Hills, returning to Wooler via Fowberry Bridge.

Places of interest along the route

A Wooler

A small market town in the shadow of the magnificent Cheviot Hills. Increasingly Wooler caters for the tourist, but is largely unspoilt, as it is primarily a centre for walking. It is the birthplace of the Dalziel brothers, the Victorian illustrators associated with Punch. At the north end of the main street is Vanessa Wallers Pottery Studio, open all year, Tuesday–Saturday and Bank Holidays 1000–1700.

B Anglo-Saxon monument, near Akeld

A monument to mark Gefrin, a 7th-century Anglo-Saxon town, where Paulinus preached the Christian word.

C Branxton

A monument marks the site of the **Battle of Flodden**, fought in 1513 and the worst of the Anglo-Scottish battles. It was here that James IV was killed, along with members of nearly every Scottish noble family. Scott's epic, *Marmion*, romanticises the battle. Nearby is Branxton Church, where James' body was taken.

D St Cuthbert's Cave

St Cuthbert's cave lies a little way to the left of the route, accessible only on foot, high on the moor ridge. It is said to have been used by Cuthbert when he worked tending sheep before he saw his vision of St Aiden and went to dedicate his life to God. The cave is now National Trust property, a quiet and little visited spot.

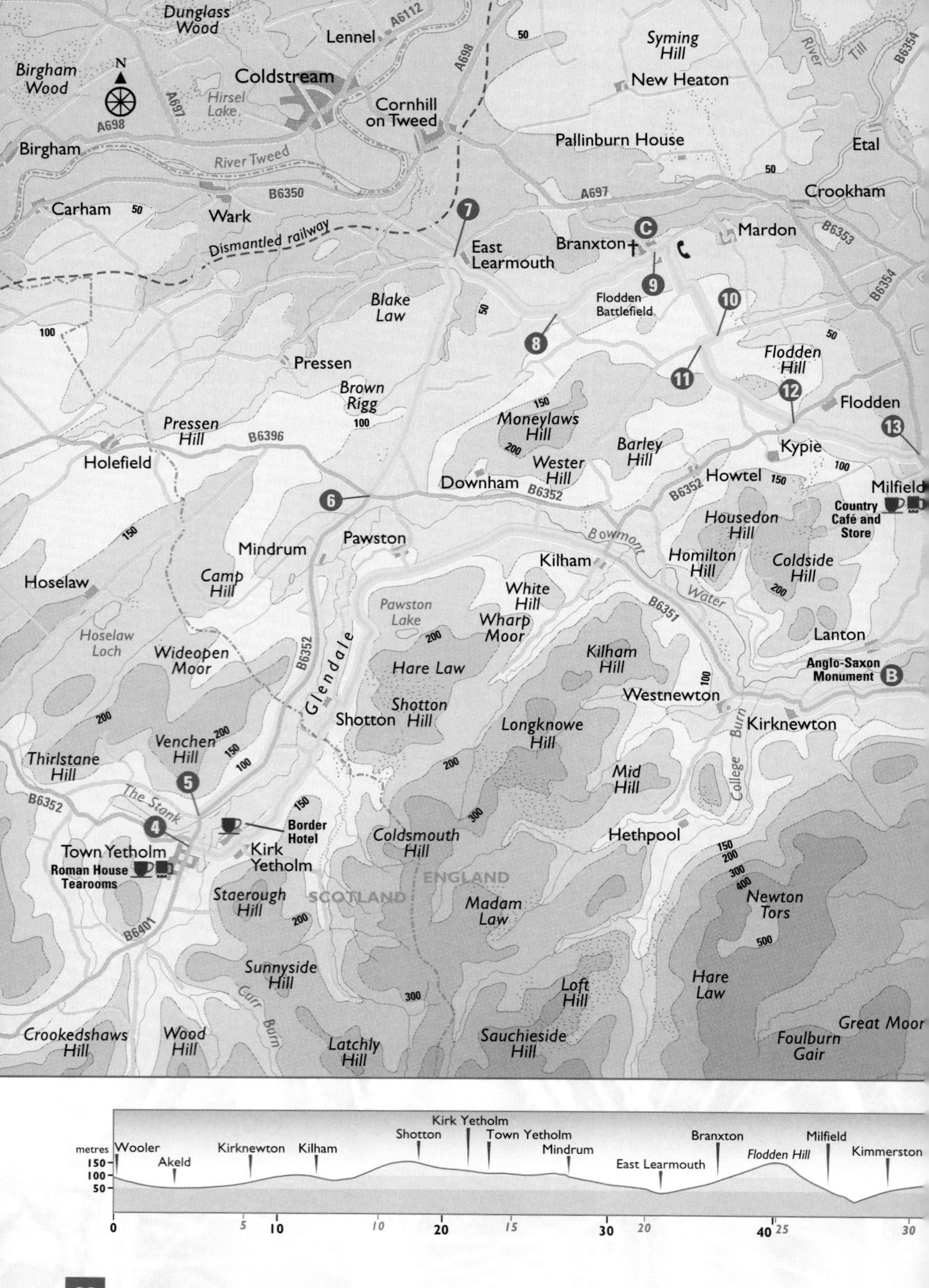
Dunglass Wood
Lennel
A6112
A698
50
Syming Hill
River Till
B6354
Birgham Wood
N
Coldstream
Hirsel Lake
A697
A698
Cornhill on Tweed
New Heaton
Birgham
River Tweed
Pallinburn House
Etal
B6350
50
A697
Crookham
Carham
50
Wark
7
C
Mardon
B6353
Dismantled railway
East Learmouth
Branxton
9
Flodden Battlefield
10
B6354
Blake Law
50
8
50
100
Pressen
11
Flodden Hill
Brown Rigg
12
Flodden
150
100
Moneylaws Hill
13
Pressen Hill
B6396
200
Barley Hill
Kypie
Holefield
Wester Hill
Howtel
150
100
Downham
B6352
B6352
Milfield
6
Country Café and Store
Housedon Hill
150
Bowmont
Pawston
Mindrum
Kilham
Homilton Hill
Coldside Hill
Hoselaw
Camp Hill
White Hill
Water
200
Pawston Lake
B6351
Wharp Moor
Lanton
Hoselaw Loch
200
Wideopen Moor
B6352
Glendale
Hare Law
Kilham Hill
Anglo-Saxon Monument
B
100
Westnewton
Shotton Hill
Shotton
Kirknewton
200
Longknowe Hill
Venchen Hill
200
150
Burn
Thirlstane Hill
100
200
Mid Hill
College
5
B6352
The Stank
150
300
Border Hotel
4
Coldsmouth Hill
Hethpool
Town Yetholm
Kirk Yetholm
150
200
Roman House Tearooms
ENGLAND
300
400
Staerough Hill
SCOTLAND
Madam Law
Newton Tors
200
B6401
500
Sunnyside Hill
Curr Burn
300
Loft Hill
Hare Law
Great Moor
Crookedshaws Hill
Wood Hill
Latchly Hill
Sauchieside Hill
Foulburn Gair
metres
150
100
50
Wooler
Akeld
Kirknewton
Kilham
Shotton
Kirk Yetholm
Town Yetholm
Mindrum
East Learmouth
Branxton
Flodden Hill
Milfield
Kimmerston
0
5
10
10
20
15
30
20
40
25
30

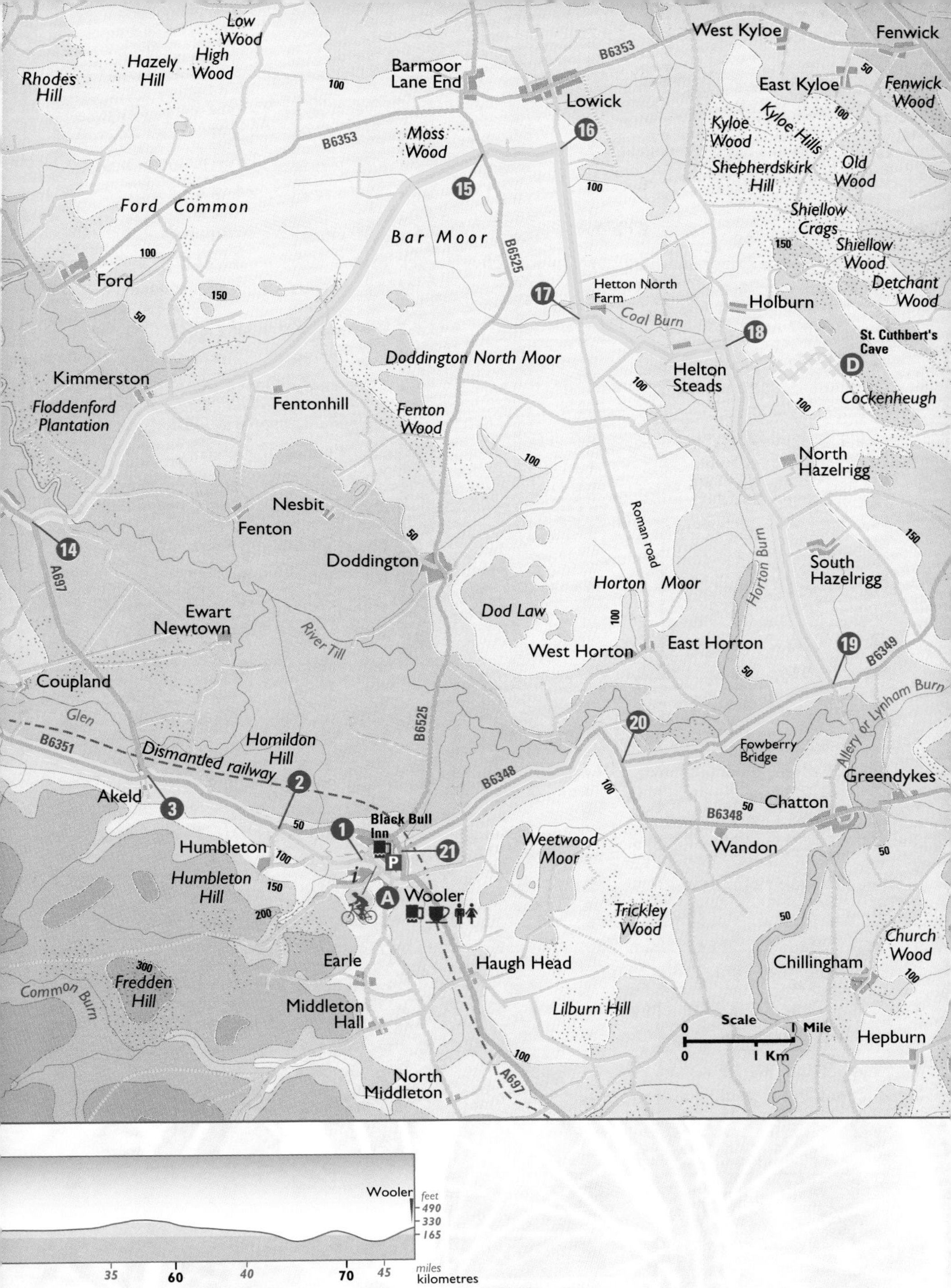

Low Wood
Hazely Hill
High Wood
Rhodes Hill
Barmoor Lane End
West Kyloe
Fenwick
B6353
East Kyloe
Fenwick Wood
Lowick
Kyloe Wood
Kyloe Hills
Moss Wood
B6353
Shepherdskirk Hill
Old Wood
Ford Common
Shiellow Crags
Bar Moor
Shiellow Wood
B6525
Detchant Wood
Ford
Hetton North Farm
Coal Burn
Holburn
St. Cuthbert's Cave
Doddington North Moor
Helton Steads
Cockenheugh
Kimmerston
Floddenford Plantation
Fentonhill
Fenton Wood
North Hazelrigg
Roman road
Nesbit
Fenton
Horton Burn
South Hazelrigg
Doddington
A697
Horton Moor
Ewart Newtown
Dod Law
River Till
West Horton
East Horton
B6349
Coupland
Allery or Lynham Burn
Glen
B6351
Dismantled railway
Homildon Hill
B6525
Fowberry Bridge
Greendykes
B6348
Akeld
Chatton
B6348
Black Bull Inn
Humbleton
Weetwood Moor
Wandon
Humbleton Hill
Wooler
Trickley Wood
Church Wood
Earle
Haugh Head
Chillingham
Common Burn
Fredden Hill
Middleton Hall
Lilburn Hill
Scale
0
1 Mile
0
1 Km
Hepburn
North Middleton
A697
Wooler
feet
490
330
165
35
60
40
70
45
miles
kilometres

Route description

Leave Wooler on the main street, with Tourist Information Centre on LHS and Black Bull Inn on RHS.

1 TL at the end of street (pottery on RHS), SP Burn House Road. Continue past Humbleton to junction with A697.

2 TL at TJ onto A697, SP Coldstream.

3 TL, SP Yeavering/Kirknewton/Yetholm. Continue as route enters Northumberland National Park along Glendale, passing site of Anglo Saxon town, into Scotland and onto Kirk Yetholm. Go over bridge into Town Yetholm.

4 TR at TJ, SP Mindrum/Kelso (22.5km/14 miles), or TL to Town Yetholm (tearoom).

5 TR, SP Wooler. Continue on this road, back along Glendale but on opposite side of river.

6 SO at XR away from B road, SP Cornhill (29.5km/18.5 miles). Continue into East Learmouth.

7 TR by pillar box, SP Branxton/Milfield (hidden in hedge). ***33.5km (21 miles)***

8 TL, SP Branxton/Crookham. Continue, passing monument to Battle of Flodden on RHS, Branxton Church on LHS.

9 TR at TJ, into Branxton. TR in village by telephone box. Go up steep hill and continue to TJ.

10 TR at TJ, SP Crookham. Continue past Branxton Moor Farm and cottages.

11 TL up hill, SP Milfield/Wooler (40km/25 miles). Continue to XR.

12 SO at XR, SP Milfield/Wooler. Enjoy descent, but take care as you approach A697.

13 TR at TJ onto A697 and continue through Milfield.

14 At the end of village, TL, SP Doddington/Fenton/Kimmerston/Woodbridge. Follow this road as it climbs through Kimmerston onto Ford Common.

Food and drink

Plenty of choice in Wooler in summer (and a fine fish and chip shop).

Tankerville Arms Hotel, Wooler
On the A697 at the bottom of the town, and always reliable for a good meal.

Border Hotel, Kirk Yetholm
Popular with walkers on the Pennine Way as they pass through the village.

Romany House Tearooms, Town Yetholm
Only open in summer, located in a lovely situation overlooking a small lake.

Country Café and Store, Milfield
Recommended, although it can be busy with coach parties. Open all year for teas, cakes and hot meals.

15 SO at XR, no SP but white bungalow. ***54km (33.5 miles)***

16 TR at TJ, no SP but coast ahead and village of Lowick (several silver silos) to left. Continue, ignoring two TL (first SP Moorhouse, second SP Laverock Law).

17 TL at XR, no SP (58km/36 miles). Continue SO to follow road past Hetton North Farm and through Hetton Steads.

18 TR at TJ, SP Belford/Chatton. Continue.

19 TR at XR, SP Fowberry Bridge ahead (66km/41 miles). Go over bridge and up hill to junction with B6348.

20 TR at TJ onto B6348, SP Wooler (there is often a flock of black sheep in field at this junction). Enjoy descent past Weetwood Bridge and continue into Wooler.

21 SO at XR with A697, up Church Street and return to car park to complete the route. ***74km (46 miles)***

Route 21

CAMBO, ROTHBURY AND ELSDON

Route information

Distance 74km (46 miles)

Grade Strenuous

Terrain Quiet and hilly roads.

Time to allow 10 hours.

Getting there by car Cambo is a small village, off the A696 Newcastle/Jedburgh road, at the junction of the B6343 and B6342. Cambo is 1km (0.6 mile) from Wallington Hall, an alternative start point. There is car parking in Cambo.

Getting there by train There is no practical railway access to the route.

A hard but rewarding ride. From Cambo, often overlooked as visitors head for Wallington Hall, the route climbs north past Rothley Crags and up through the Simsonside Hills to Rothbury, an ancient market town popular with walkers and fishermen. The hills are less steep for a few miles as you climb away from Rothbury, through Harbottle and on, following the River Coquet into Elsdon. A final climb takes you over the moors and past the infamous Winters Gibbet before following a flattish road back to Cambo. The views are superb.

Places of interest along the route

A Codger Fort

A ruin, clearly seen to the right of the route as it leaves Rothley Crags. Standing out against the moorland, Codger Fort was once an important feature of border warfare.

B Tosson Tower, near Great Tosson

On the left hand side of the route, as it descends into the hamlet of Great Tosson, stands Tosson Tower. A Pele tower, now ruined, it has a useful information board for visitors. The tower was built 600 years ago as a fortified home for the Northumberland Ogle family. Open to the public during daylight hours.

C Rothbury

The capital of Coquetdale, this ancient market town is popular with walkers and fishermen. The town sits on the banks of the River Coquet and is bordered by the Simonside Hills. Look out for the Victorian street lamps. **Cragside House** was built between 1864 and 1884 for Lord Armstrong, and during 1869 the house became the first to be list be electricity generated by water pwoer. The gardens are fantastic, with a series of small lakes created for the hydraulic power generation. National Trust property. House open April to October, Tuesday–Sunday 1300–1730; daily in June. Gardens open April to October, Tuesday–Sunday 1030–1900; June, daily 1030–1900; November and December, weekends 1030–1600; also open Bank Holidays. Charge. Telephone (01669) 620333. Lady's Well, Holystone, is traditionally associated with St

Peat Law
Gills Law
Cold Law
Scrainwood
Yetlington
Crosshill
Callaly
Thrunton Wood
Newtown
Elilaw
Biddlestone
Netherton Northside
Follions
Lorbottle Hall
Coe Hill
Lords Seat
Netherton
Netherton Burnfoot
Lorbottle
Coe Crags
Long Crag
River Alwin
Alwinton
Biddlestone Edge
Burradon
Bankhead
Edlingham Burn
Rimside Moor
Swallow Knowe
High Trewhitt
Whittle
Back Burn
Cartington
Debdon
Debdon Burn
Coquet Crafts Café
Harbottle
West Wood
Foxton Burn
Sharperton Edge
Sandylands
Barrow Hill
Barrow Burn
Harbottle Hills
Harbottle Hill
Wood Hall
Sharperton
Plainfield
Wreigh Burn
Snitter
Debdon Whitefield
Shirlaw Pike
Forest
Warton
Debdon Lake
Black Burn
High Farnham
Flotterton
Thropton
Sun Kitchen
High Linn
Harbottle Crag
Holystone
Low Farnham
Rothbury
Nelly's Moss Lakes
Blackburn Lake
Bloody Moss
Highspoon Hill
Holystone Common
Caistron
River Coquet
Ryehill
Allerdene
Hope
Little Tosson
Whitton
Cragend
North Yardhope
Holystone Burn
Great Tosson
Newtown
Hepple
B6341
Healey
Wolfershiel
B6344
The Beacon
Dod Hill
Harehaugh
Bickerton
Tosson Tower
B6342
Pauperhaugh
Long Hill
West Row
Swindon
East Row
Keenshaw Burn
Ravens Heugh
Simonside
Bashygap
Tosson Hill
Simonside Hills
Black Stitchel
The Lee
Black Hill
Grasslees Burn
Weather Head
Rothbury
Low Hesleyhurst
Grasslees
Sandy Crags
Whitefield Hill
Selby's Cove
Forest Burn
Darden Burn
Gunners Box
Forestburn Gate
Maglin Burn
Billsmoor Park
High Rigg
Spylaw Burn

Leighton Hill
Colwellhill
Elsdon Burn
Elsdon
Cyclists' Café
13
14
D
Monkridge
Raylees
Wether Hill
Hunterlee Hill
Raylees Common
Blaxter Lough
Black Burn
Lykenook
Middle Hill
Wishaw Pike
East Woodburn Common
Lisle's Burn
A68
Chesterhope
Stiddlehill Common
Ridsdale
Hepple Heugh
Chesterhope Common
Aid Moss
Scale
0
1 Mile
0
1 Km
Sweethope Loughs
Curtis Burn
River Wansbeck
Darden Lough
Little Lough
Dough Crag
Harwood
King's Dod
Tod Knowe
Forest
Eastnook
Harry's Wood
Battle Hill
Steng Moss
15
E
Winters Gibbet
Harwood Head
Ottercops Moss
A696
Ottercops Burn
Whaup Moss
Raechester
Catcherside
Chesters
Blackhalls
Knowesgate
Ray Fell
West Whitehill
Kirkwhelpington
Cornhills
Northside
Kirkharle
B6342
Lough Hill
Newbiggin Burn
Fallowlees Lough
Hemmel Hill
Fallowlees Burn
Fontburn Reservoir
16
Rothley Lakes
Dolf Burn
Kirkhill
Hart Burn
Codger Fort
A
Rothley
Scots' Gap
B6343
1
17
Cambo
Wallington Hall
F
Swilder Burn
Coldrife
Coltpark
Wingates
River Font
Ritton
Nunnykirk
Clayton Fell
Newpark Wood
Ewesley Burn
Netherwitton
Bellion
Longwitton
Oldpark Wood
Wittonstone
Longwitton Dene
Hartburn
High Angerton
Middleton
Marlish
River Wansbeck
Low Angerton
Middleton Bank Top
Bolam
Bolam Lake

Ninian. National Trust property. Free access at all reasonable times. Telephone (01670) 774691.

D Elsdon

Once the capital of Redesdale and the most lawless place in Northumberland, now a quiet village surrounded by moorland. It boasts a fortified tower built in 1400 and a notable 14th-century church. The village green provides a peaceful spot for a rest before the final climb.

E Winters Gibbet

On the RHS of the route, clearly visible at the top of the climb out of Elsdon, is a traditional hangman's noose, with a suspended stone head. It provides an eerie reminder of the fate of those condemned in former times.

F Wallington Hall, Cambo

Set in 40.5ha (100 acres) of lawns, lakes and woodland, the house dates from 1688 and features plasterwork, collections of porcelain and dolls houses and a Museum of Curiosities. National Trust property. Tearoom, shop and plant centre. House open April to September, Wednesday–Monday 1300–1730; October, Wednesday–Monday 1300–1630. Walled garden open daily, April to September 1000–1900; October 1000–1800; November to March 1000–1600. Tearoom and shop open April to September, daily 1030–1730; October, Wednesday–Monday 1030–1700; November and December, Wednesday–Sunday 1200–1600. Telephone (01670) 774283.

Route description

Start by the post office in Cambo. Leave village on minor road (church on RHS). TR at TJ onto B6343. Continue to Scots' Gap.

1 TL onto minor road, SP Rothley/Rothbury. Continue on this road past Rothley Crags, SO at Rothley XR and past Codger Fort. Continue SO as road climbs and dips on some fairly stiff inclines.

2 TL onto minor road, SP Simonside, also Northumberland National Park boundary stone (14.5km/9 miles). Follow this minor road along edge of forest to Great Tosson, with views of Coquet valley.

3 TR down hill at TJ (Tosson Tower is on left, telephone box opposite).

4 TR at TJ, SP Newtown/Rothbury. Take next TL to descend into Rothbury.

5 TL at TJ, over bridge into town centre. TL at TJ, up main street. Follow this road (B6341) out of Rothbury and continue with River Coquet on left into Thropton.

6 TR by Cross Keys pub, SP Netherton/Trewhitt/Snitter. ***26km (16 miles)***

7 TL and continue through Snitter to Netherton.

8 Pass fish ladder at entrance to

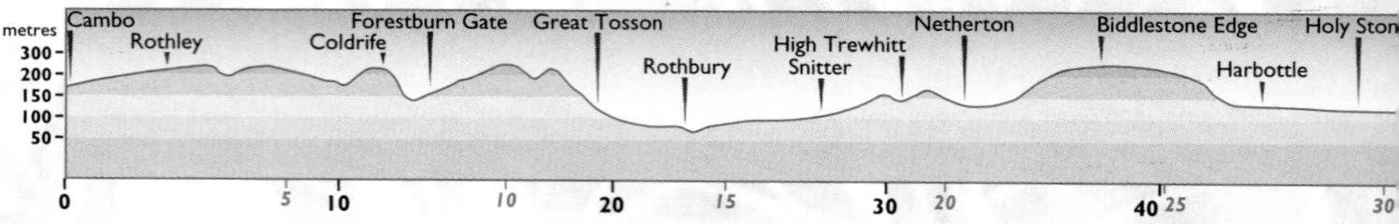

Netherton (33.5km/21 miles). Continue through Netherton, following road towards Alwinton and Harbottle.

9 TL at TJ (just before Alwinton, away from white post and rail bridge).

41.5km (26 miles)

10 Continue through Harbottle.

11 TR (just before Sharperton), SP Elsdon/Holystone.

12 TR at TJ onto major road, SP Elsdon/Otterburn (51.5km/32 miles). Continue into Elsdon.

13 TL in front of pub, SP Morpeth/Newcastle (59.5km/37 miles). Then, TR at TJ, SP Morpeth/Newcastle (ensure you take this road out of village).

14 Continue on this road out of village, SP Harwood/Cambo/Morpeth.

15 Pass Winters Gibbet on RHS. There are superb views over Tyneside.

64km (40 miles)

16 TR at TJ onto B6342, SP Cambo/Hexham.

17 To visit Wallington Hall, continue SO. Otherwise, TL into Cambo, SP Cambo PO and shop, and finish the ride.

74km (46 miles)

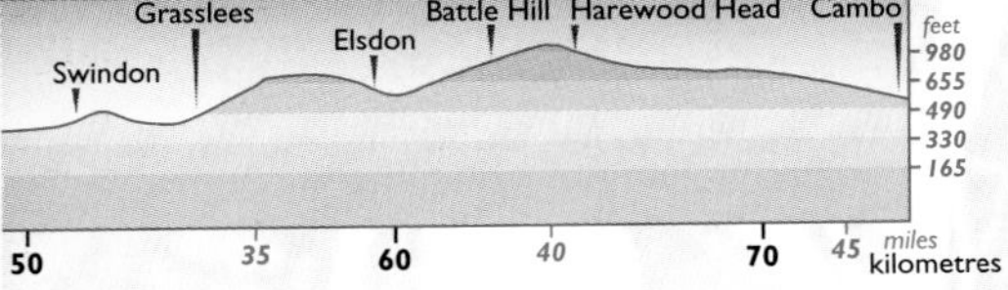

Food and drink

There is a wide choice of pubs, cafés and hotels in Rothbury, a pub and tearoom in Elsdon and a tearoom at Wallington Hall. However, no cafés and pubs are guaranteed to be open elsewhere, so you should carry food and drink to sustain you during the ride.

Sun Kitchen, Rothbury
Recommended for good home-cooked meals and snacks.

Coquet Crafts Café, Harbottle
Located in the Post Office and shop.

Cyclists' Café, Elsdon
The traditional cyclists' stop in Elsdon – in the front room of a house near a telephone box and recognised by the bicycles propped against the porch wall. Great cyclists' food – pasta, and lots of hot tea. Often busy on Wednesdays and Sundays.

Route **22**

HADRIAN'S WALL – VINDOLANDA, HOUSESTEADS AND BIRDOSWALD

Route information

Distance 75.5km (47 miles)

Grade Strenuous

Terrain On-road, with some stiff climbs and exposure to strong winds at the high points.

Time to allow 6–8 hours.

Getting there by car Park at Bardon Mill Station, just off the A69, Newcastle/Hexham road.

Getting there by train Bardon Mill station is on the Newcastle/Carlisle line. Telephone (0345) 484950 for travel information.

This ride takes in some of the best Roman remains in Northumberland. In addition, at the western extreme, the route passes 12th-century Lannercost Priory. From Bardon Mill the route climbs straight out of the Tyne valley, past Chesterholme to Greenhead, following the Roman wall down to the pastureland of Cumbria and Walton. The figure of eight route means a final stiff climb back through Greenhead before a descent into Haltwhistle to follow quiet roads along the Tyne valley back to Bardon Mill. Many of the places of interest along the route are closed during the winter months. Hadrian's Wall can be bleak, so do choose a good day unless you really do want to recreate the misery of being a Roman soldier in northern Britain.

To explore all of the Roman remains along this route you may want to do the ride over two days. Accommodation is available at Greenhead (hotel or Youth hostel) and in Brampton, just to the west of the ride. Telephone Haltwhistle Tourist Information Centre (01434 322002) for information on accommodation.

Route description

Leave Bardon Mill station car park and go up short drive to main street. TR to leave village.

1 TL at end of village, uphill and under A69, SP Westwood. Keep left, SP Westwood.

2 TL down hill at XR, SP Bardon Mill. Continue over bridge and TR, SP Vindolanda.

3 TR at TJ, SP Vindolanda. Pass TR for Vindolanda (single track road).

4 Arrive TJ with B6318 (Once Brewed National Park Visitor Centre on LHS). To visit Housesteads, TR at TJ. Otherwise, to continue route, TL at TJ and continue along B3618 over Haltwhistle Common.

5 TR to visit Roman Army Museum (24km/15 miles). Otherwise, continue on B6318, down hill into Greenhead.

6 Keep right at end of village and follow B6318 into Gilsland.

Hadrian's Wall

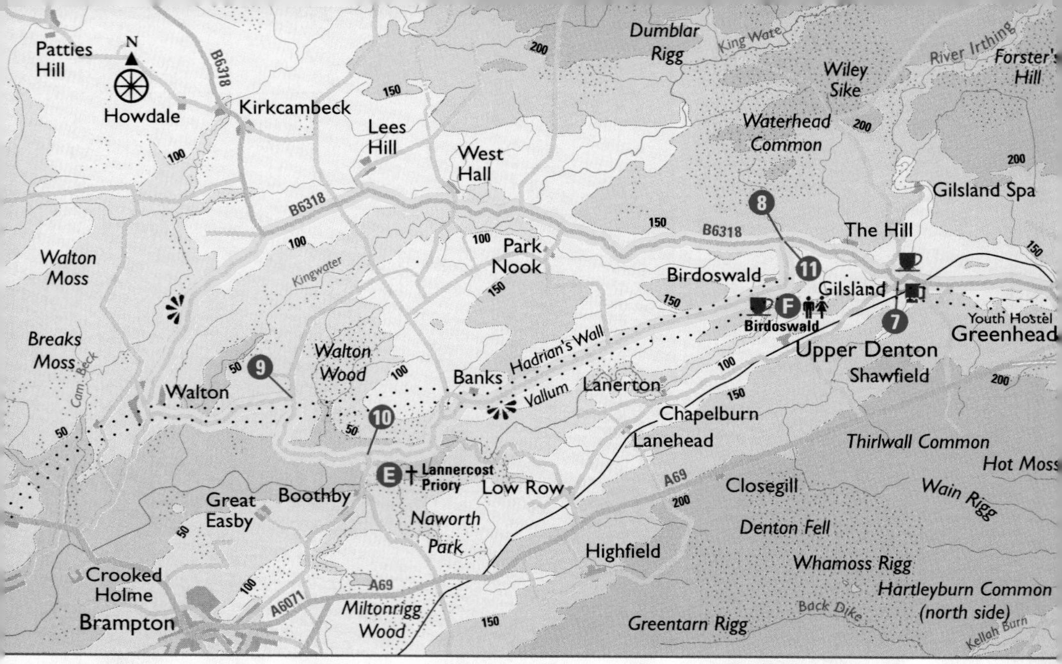

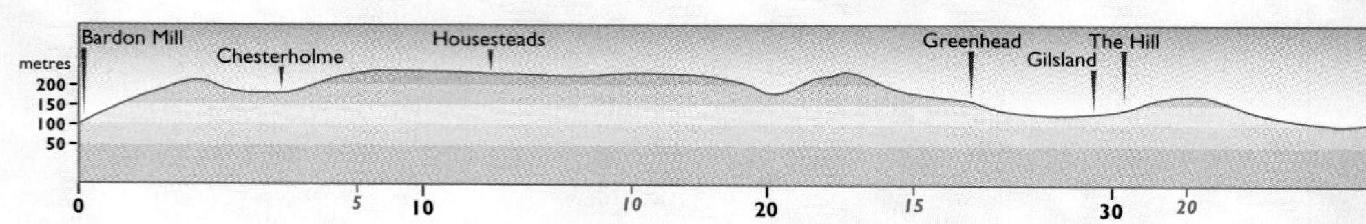

7 TR at TJ, staying on B6318 (29.5km/18.5 miles). Cross bridge. TL (staying on B6318), SP Roadhead/Langholme/Hadrian's Wall.

8 Continue on B6318 which becomes country lane through pastureland. Ignore all turns until road forks. Take LHF (away from B6318), SP Walton/Brampton (40km/25 miles). Follow this lane (views of Cumbrian hills) into Walton. TL at Centurion Inn, marked by old metal finger post SP Lannercost.

9 TR at TJ, SP Lannercost Priory.

10 To visit Lannercost Priory, TR at TJ and immediately TL over cattle grid. Otherwise, SO to continue route, along Irthing Valley for climb up to Banks (views of Tyne valley). Follow this road (beside long sections of Hadrian's Wall). Pass TR for Birdoswald (55.5km/34.5 miles). Continue to TJ with B6318.

11 TR into Gilsland. Then, TL, SP Greenhead, and follow this road into Greenhead (62km/38.5 miles). Continue through Greenhead and up steep hill. Roman Army Museum is on left at top of hill.

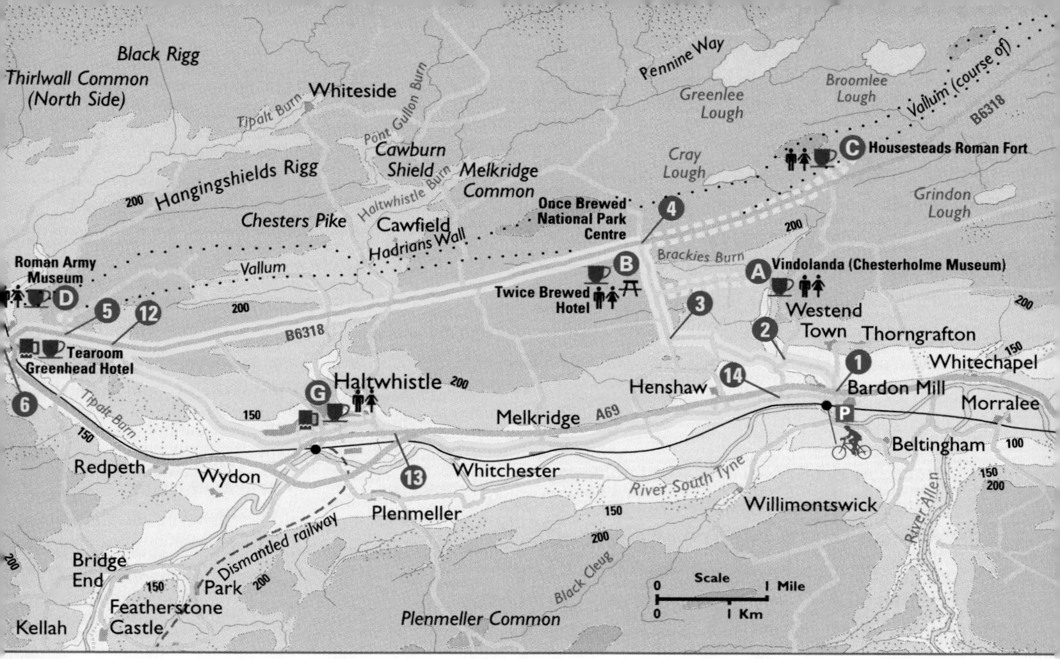

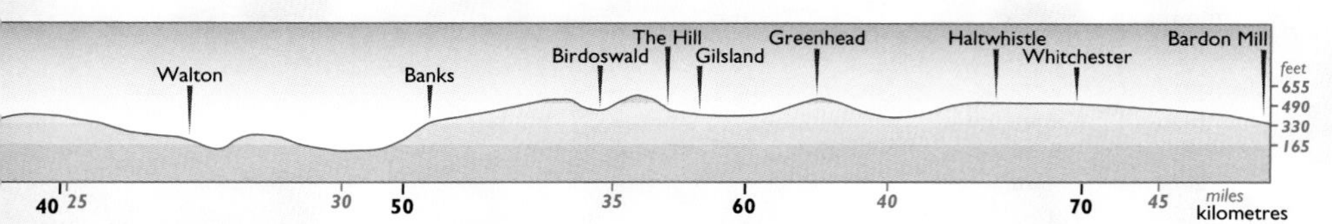

12 TR, SP Haltwhistle (63.5km/39.5 miles). Descend into Haltwhistle and bear left into main street. Continue through Haltwhistle.

13 TR at TJ and immediately TL under main road, SP Melkridge. Continue on this quiet road along Tyne valley, with river and railway to right and main road to left.

14 TR at TJ (away from main road) into Bardon Mill. The tall pottery chimney signals the end of the route, with a last TR into station car park. ***75.5km (47 miles)***

Places of interest along the route

A Vindolanda, Chesterholme Museum, Bardon Mill

The remains of a Roman fort and settlement. The excavated finds are displayed in the museum, together with descriptions of daily life and full-scale replicas of the Roman buildings. Also lovely gardens. Coffee shop. Open as per the Roman Army Museum (see D). Charge (discount to English Heritage members). Telephone (01434) 344277.

B Once Brewed National Park Centre, Bardon Mill

The visitor centre contains exhibitions and a shop and gives easy access onto Hadrian's Wall. Open daily, March to June 0930–1700; July and August 0930–1800; September and October 0930–1700; November, weekends only 1000–1500. Admission free. Telephone (01434) 344396.

C Housesteads Roman Fort, Haydon Bridge

The site of the best preserved Roman fort and the only surviving example of a Roman hospital in the country. Operated jointly by English Heritage and the National Trust. Visitor centre, tearoom and shop. Open daily, April to September 1000–1800; October 1000–1700; November–March 1000–1600. Charge. Telephone (01434) 344363.

D Roman Army Museum, near Greenheads

The museum describes the life of a Roman soldier through reconstructions and audio commentaries. Coffee shop. Open March to November, daily 1000–1600 (telephone to confirm early and late season). Charge (discount to English Heritage members). Telephone (01434 344060.

E Lannercost Priory

Church and ruins of the Augustinian priory (English Heritage), founded in 1166 and abandoned during the dissolution of the monasteries in 1536. Local guides are on site during the summer. Church open all year, daily 1000–1730. Priory open daily, April to September 1000–1800. Telephone (01697) 73030.

F Birdoswald

Roman fort and visitor centre, offering an insight into life on the Roman frontier. Café accessible without entering the museum. Open March to November, daily 1000–1700. Charge (discount to English Heritage members). Telephone (01697) 747602.

G Haltwhistle

A traditional market town, recently established as the centre of the country. There has been a settlement here since the 2nd century, when the Romans arrived and started construction of Hadrian's Wall. Two sections of the wall have been excavated in Haltwhistle. Walltown Crags comprises a section of wall and turret. Winshields comprises the highest point on the wall and an unexcavated milecastle. Free access to both sites at all reasonable times. Telephone the Tourist Information Centre for further information on (01434) 322002.

Food and drink

There are pubs and tearooms in Gilsland and Haltwhistle. Refreshments are also available at Vindolanda, Housesteads, the Roman Army Museum and Birdoswald.

Twice Brewed Hotel

Adjacent to Once Brewed Visitor Centre, offering a limited range of hot drinks and snacks. Parties must telephone ahead.

Greenhead Tearoom, Greenhead

Open daily all year, for teas, coffees and snacks.

Greenhead Hotel, Greenhead

Bar meals available 1200–1500 and from 1900 every evening (also accommodation).

Route 23

BAMBURGH, ALNWICK AND ROS CASTLE

Route information

Distance 80.5km (50 miles)

Grade Moderate

Terrain Undulating roads across rolling hills. There is one stiff climb towards the end of the route.

Time to allow 5–8 hours.

Getting there by car Brownieside is just off the A1, north of Alnwick. Park by the Little Chef.

Getting there by train There is a limited train service to Chathill. Telephone (0345) 484950 for travel information. To join the route, TR out of station and continue to direction 9.

This ride samples all that is typical of Northumberland: castles, the seaside, a pele tower and moorland. A gentle start from Brownieside takes you north to the coast, with dramatic views of Bamburgh Castle. On along the coast to Seahouses (access the Farne Islands from here), before cutting inland to Alnwick. A stiff ride towards Wooler and a turn before Chillingham, take you up and over the Ros Castle road. The climb brings rewards with the fabulous views of the coast and the descent back to Brownieside. There are few pubs/cafés on the last stretch so it is worth gathering provisions in Alnwick for the last 32km (20 miles). If you want to visit places of interest along the way you may want to make this a two day ride, in which case Alnwick is a convenient mid-way point. Telephone the Tourist Information Centre for details on (01665) 510665.

Route description

TR out of Little Chef car park, along old A1 (Mason's Arms pub on RHS). TL (immediately before TJ) and through underpass under A1. Take care and watch out for agricultural vehicles using underpass.

1 TL at end of tunnel. Continue past silos. SO at XR, SP Ellingham.

2 Arrive Ellingham. Take second TL, SP Newham/Lucker. TL at TJ (Pack Horse pub on RHS).

3 TL at TJ, SP trunk road A1. Go over bridge and TR, SP Newham Hagg. Continue along this gated road with grass down centre, through Newham Hagg and TR at TJ.

4 SO at XR, SP Lucker 1. Continue to TJ by memorial cross.

5 TR at TJ (9.5km/6 miles). Then, TR at TJ, SP Bamburgh B1341. Continue into Bamburgh with views of castle.

6 TR at TJ to leave Bamburgh with castle on LHS (15km/9.5 miles). Continue along coast into Seahouses. Farne Islands clearly visible on LHS.

7 TR at first roundabout, SP Alnwick. SO at second roundabout, SP North Sunderland. Continue through West Fleetham.

8 TR at TJ, SP Chathill (27km/17 miles). This is part of the National Cycle Route. Go over

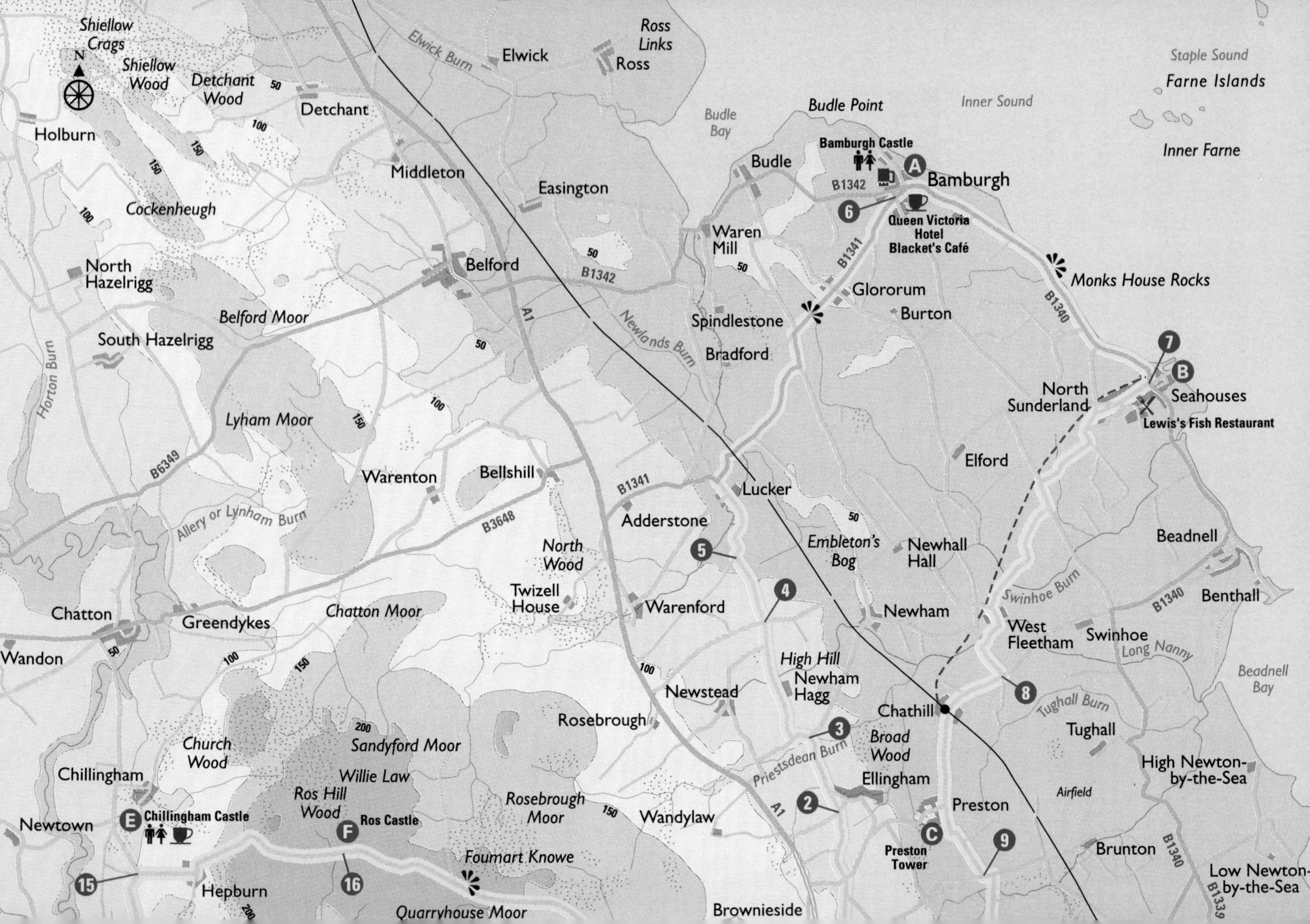

N
Shiellow Crags
Shiellow Wood
Detchant Wood
Detchant
Holburn
Elwick
Elwick Burn
Ross Links
Ross
Budle Point
Budle Bay
Inner Sound
Staple Sound
Farne Islands
Inner Farne
Bamburgh Castle
Bamburgh
Budle
B1342
Queen Victoria Hotel
Blacket's Café
Middleton
Easington
Cockenheugh
Waren Mill
B1341
Glororum
Burton
Monks House Rocks
B1340
North Hazelrigg
Belford
B1342
Belford Moor
South Hazelrigg
Spindlestone
Bradford
Newlands Burn
A1
Horton Burn
North Sunderland
Seahouses
Lewis's Fish Restaurant
Lyham Moor
Warenton
Bellshill
Elford
Lucker
B6349
B1341
Adderstone
Allery or Lynham Burn
B3648
North Wood
Embleton's Bog
Newhall Hall
Beadnell
Twizell House
Warenford
Newham
Swinhoe Burn
Benthall
B1340
Chatton
Greendykes
Chatton Moor
West Fleetham
Swinhoe
Long Nanny
Wandon
High Hill
Newham Hagg
Newstead
Beadnell Bay
Rosebrough
Chathill
Tughall Burn
Church Wood
Sandyford Moor
Broad Wood
Tughall
Chillingham
Willie Law
Priestsdean Burn
Ellingham
High Newton-by-the-Sea
Ros Hill Wood
Rosebrough Moor
Preston
Airfield
Newtown
Chillingham Castle
Ros Castle
Wandylaw
Preston Tower
Brunton
Foumart Knowe
Low Newton-by-the-Sea
Hepburn
Quarryhouse Moor
Brownieside
B1339

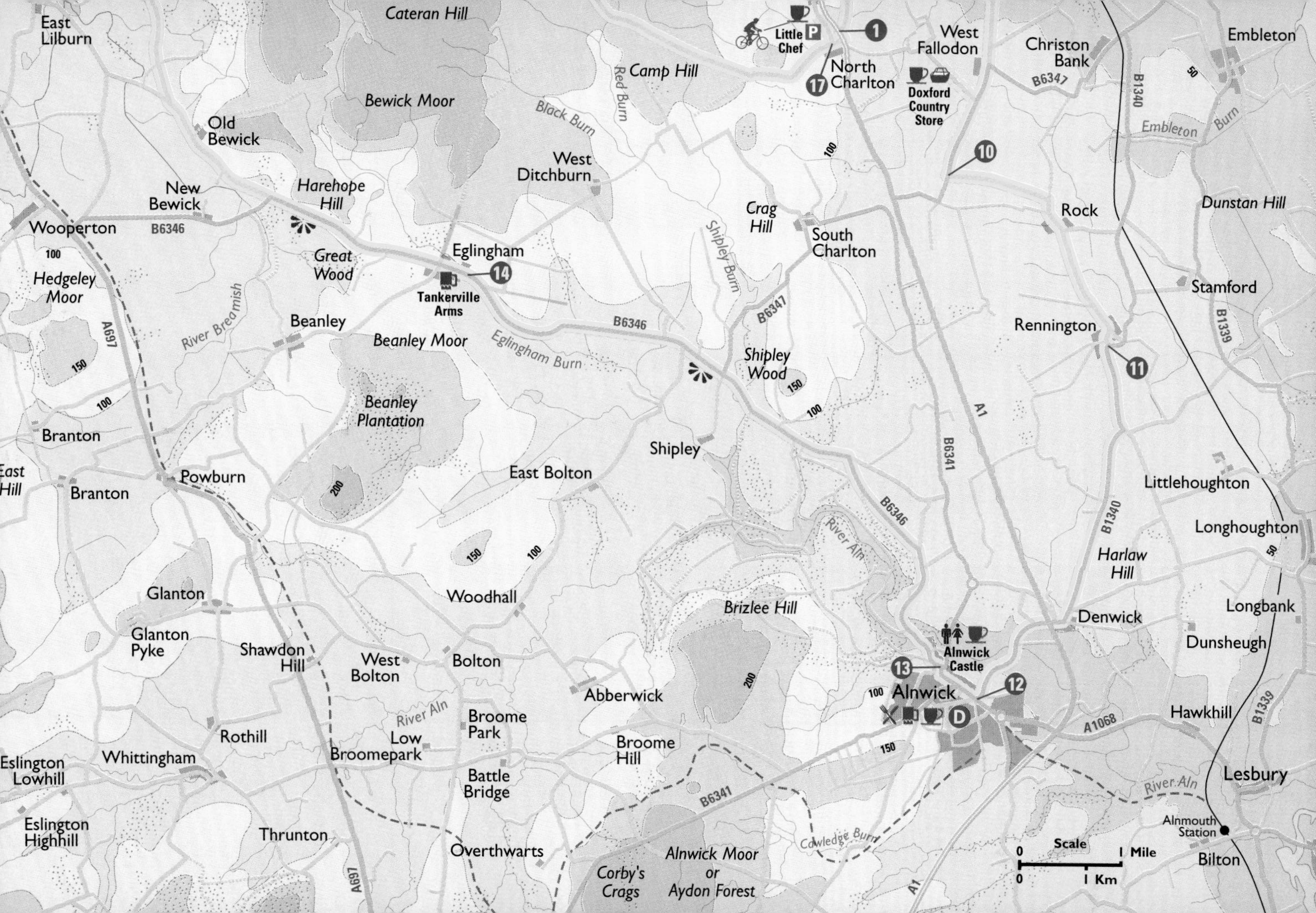

East Lilburn
Cateran Hill
Little Chef
North Charlton
West Fallodon
Christon Bank
Embleton
Doxford Country Store
Camp Hill
Red Burn
Bewick Moor
Black Burn
B6347
B1340
Embleton Burn
Old Bewick
West Ditchburn
New Bewick
Harehope Hill
Crag Hill
Rock
Dunstan Hill
Wooperton
B6346
Eglingham
South Charlton
Shipley Burn
Great Wood
Tankerville Arms
Stamford
Hedgeley Moor
B1339
A697
River Breamish
Beanley
Beanley Moor
Eglingham Burn
Rennington
Shipley Wood
Beanley Plantation
A1
Branton
Shipley
B6341
East Hill
Powburn
East Bolton
Littlehoughton
Longhoughton
River Aln
Harlaw Hill
Glanton
Woodhall
Brizlee Hill
Longbank
Denwick
Glanton Pyke
Shawdon Hill
West Bolton
Bolton
Alnwick Castle
Dunsheugh
Abberwick
Alnwick
Broome Park
Hawkhill
A1068
Rothill
Low Broomepark
Broome Hill
Eslington Lowhill
Whittingham
Battle Bridge
Lesbury
Eslington Highhill
Thrunton
Overthwarts
Cawledge Burn
Alnmouth Station
Alnwick Moor or Aydon Forest
Corby's Crags
Scale
0 1 Mile
0 1 Km
Bilton

Chathill station crossings. Pass Preston Tower on RHS.

9 Follow the road round corner to left (31.5km/19.5 miles). Then, TR, SP Doxford Country Store. Continue through West Fallodon, passing TR to Doxford Country Store.

10 TL, SP Rock 1/Rennington 2. Continue through Rock and Rennington.

11 TR at TJ, SP Denwick/Alnwick. Continue through Denwick, over A1 and into Alnwick.

12 TR at TJ with monument (45.5km/ 28.5 miles), through gate to town centre. Then, take RHF, SP Alnwick Castle, continue in front of Woolworth's and down Narrowgate.

13 TL in front of castle onto B6346, along Balifgate, down Cannogate and out of Alnwick over River Aln (Hulne Abbey on LHS). Follow this road along Hulne Park boundary wall and on to Eglingham. Views of Cheviot Hills.

14 Continue through Eglingham (57km/ 35.5 miles) and past Old Bewick Cross on RHS.

15 To visit Chillingham Castle, continue SO. Otherwise, to continue route TR, SP Hepburn/ Hepburn Wood Walks. ***66.5km (41.5 miles)***

16 SO for steep climb over cattle grid and onto moorland around Ros Castle. Continue on this high, gated road, until it descends to TJ with A1.

17 TL at TJ (immediately before A1) and continue along this stretch of old A1 back to Brownieside Little Chef and the end of the route. ***80.5km (50 miles)***

Places of interest along the route

Ⓐ Bamburgh

A picturesque village dominated by **Bamburgh Castle** set on the promontory of the Great Whin Sill. The castle was first constructed as a modest wooden structure in 547, when Bamburgh was a royal city and centre of the ancient kingdom of Bernicia. The castle was rebuilt of stone at the end of the Norman period, to resist invasion from the Scots. It is now the home of the Armstrong family and houses the Armstrong Museum dedicated to the achievements of the engineer, shipbuilder and industrialist the 1st Lord Armstrong. Tearoom. Open April to October, daily 1300–1630. Charge. Telephone (01668) 214515. Grace Darling was born in Bamburgh in 1815 and gained fame through the rescue of nine survivors from the wrecked *Forfarshire*. The **Grace Darling Museum** tells the story of the rescue and displays many original relics. Open April to October, Monday–Saturday 1000–1700, Sunday 1200–1700. Admission free. Telephone (01668) 214465.

Ⓑ Seahouses

The village was founded around the harbour, built in 1889, and now caters for the tourist. The **Marine Life Centre and Fishing Museum** houses a sea water aquarium, fisherman's cottage and exhibition area. Open all year but telephone to confirm as times vary. Charge. Telephone (01665) 721257. The **Farne Islands** (National Trust) are a small group of 28 islands 3–8km (2–5 miles) off the Northumberland

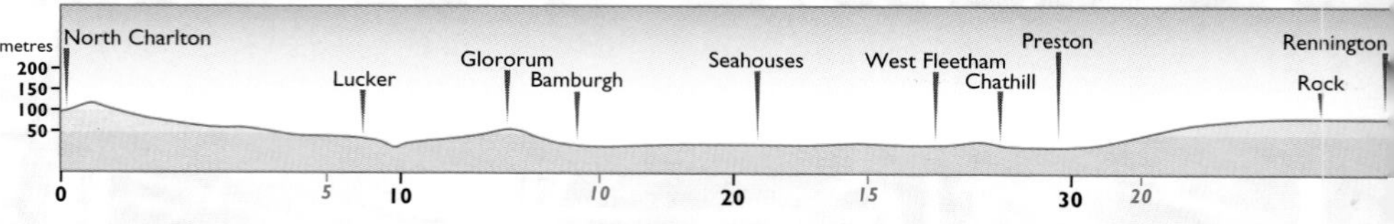

Bamburgh Castle

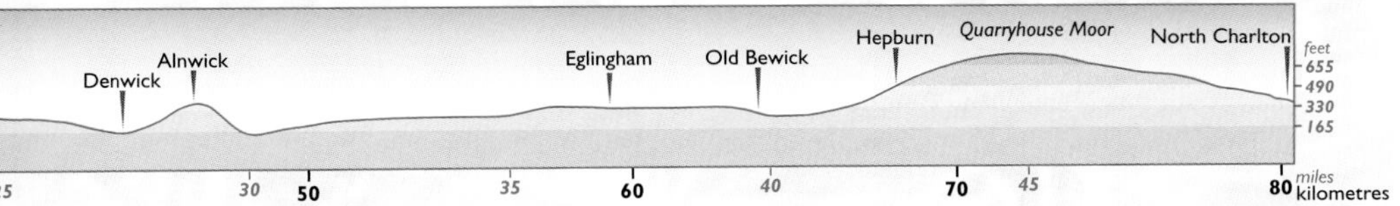

coast, forming part of the most easterly section of the Great Whin Sill. They are famous as a place of retreat for both St Aiden and St Cuthbert and as a bird reserve holding around 55,000 pairs of breeding birds of more than 21 species. The islands are also home to a colony of grey seals. Various boat trips are offered from Seahouses, weather permitting. Telephone the Tourist Information Centre for details on (01665) 720884.

C Preston Tower

This modest pele tower, constructed by Robert Harbottle c.1392, is privately owned and set in beautiful tranquil grounds. Two turrets remain and are furbished as they would have been during the 1400s. Open all year, during daylight hours. Nominal charge.

D Alnwick

The history of Alnwick is intertwined with that of the Percy family. Visitors to the town can see the Percy lions, one on top of the Tenantry Tower (on the left as the route enters the town) the other on Lion Bridge to the north of the town. **Alnwick Castle** has been home to the Percys, Dukes of Northumberland since 1309. The castle is set in magnificent grounds and contains art treasures and various exhibitions. Tearoom. Open Easter to September, daily 1100–1700. Charge. Telephone (01665) 510777. Do not miss **Barter Books** in the old station, one of the largest second hand bookshops in the country, with model trains, a real fire and tea and coffee available. Open daily, 0900–1700. Telephone (01665) 604888. The **House of Hardy Museum** illustrates the history of this company which manufactures fine fishing tackle. Visitors can see the full production cycle, with traditional crafts and skills. Open all year, Monday–Friday 0900–1700, Saturday 1000–1700; also March to October, Sunday 1330–1700. Admission free. Telephone (01665) 510027.

E Chillingham Castle, near Alnwick

This medieval fortress with 18th- and 19th-century additions contains state rooms, torture chamber, dungeon and magnificent grounds with a lake, topiary and woodland walks. Tearoom. Open May to September, Wednesday–Monday 1200–1700; daily during July and August. Charge. Telephone (01668) 215359.

F Ros Castle

On the LHS of the road, at the top of a climb and marked by SP footpath. Ros Castle was an important beacon, standing high above sea level. There are prominent earthworks and super views of the coast and Scottish hills. National Trust property. Free access at all reasonable times.

Food and drink

Alnwick has several pubs, hotels and cafés and it is worth buying refreshments here for the final part of the route.

Little Chef, Brownieside

Conveniently positioned at the start and end of the ride.

Blacket's Café, Bamburgh

Open daily Easter–October, weekends only during winter.

Queen Victoria Hotel, Bamburgh

At the top of the village. Drinks, snacks and hot meals in pleasant surroundings.

Lewis's Fish Restaurant, Seahouses

Recommended for traditional fish and chips.

Tankerville Arms, Eglingham

Open daily for bar meals, 1200–1400 and 1800–2100.

Route **24**

PONTELAND, SIMONBURN AND WARK

Route information

Distance 96.5km (60 miles)

Grade Strenuous

Terrain Tracks, lanes and minor roads. A flattish start and finish, but a hilly section midway. The off-road options are demanding and rough, requiring mountain bikes.

Time to allow 7–9 hours.

Getting there by car Ponteland is on the A696 north of Newcastle. In Ponteland, TL at traffic lights onto B6323. Park at the leisure centre on the LHS.

Getting there by train There is no practical railway access to this ride.

This route is a tour through the hamlets and villages of Northumberland's exposed moorland and sheltered valleys. From Ponteland the route heads west to Simonburn. On across the River North Tyne to Chipchase, before returning to Ponteland. Much of the route follows a section of the National Cycle Route, the Reivers Way. The optional off-road sections add 13km (8 miles) to the total distance.

Places of interest along the route

A St Mungo's Church, Simonburn

A wonderful 13th-century church built on the site of earlier Anglican and Celtic churches. It is dedicated to the 6th-century Saint Mungo who baptised and evangelised in Simonburn and founded a Christian community here. Open during daylight hours, except during worship. Donation requested. Telephone (01434) 681304.

B Chipchase Castle, Wark

One of the finest examples of Jacobean architecture in Northumberland. For 350 years the castle was the home of the Heron family, some of whom are buried in the chancel of St Mungo's. In 1621 Cuthbert Heron added a manor house to the original stone towers. Today visitors can see the chapel, 14th-century pele tower, walled vegetable and wild gardens. Castle open June, daily 1400–1700. Gardens open April to July, Thursday–Sunday 1000–1700; also open Bank Holidays. Charge. Telephone (01434) 230203.

Food and drink

Ponteland has numerous pubs and several restaurants. There is also a traditional cyclists' café in the town, on the RHS of the A696, just before the traffic lights. There are pubs in Stamfordham, Barrasford, Humshaugh and Wark, Simonburn has a shop and a tearoom and there is a tearoom and pub in Matfen.

George Hotel, Chollerford

A well-known establishment serving a high standard of drinks, bar and restaurant meals.

Village Hall, Capheaton

A 1930s style tearoom in the village hall. Open weekends only.

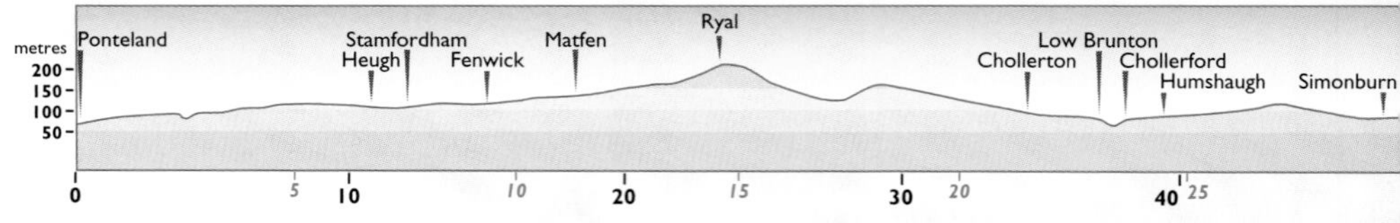

Route description

TL out of Ponteland leisure centre, onto B6323 for 200m. TR onto bridleway, SP 10. At next two XR, TL, SP 10. SO at third XR (junction with road), no SP. Continue through small estate of red brick houses to cross road and follow SP Reivers, behind shops and back onto bridleway, SP 10. Continue to TJ with road.

1 TR at TJ and immediately TL onto bridleway, SP 10. TR at junction, SP 10, and continue to junction with road. TL onto road, no SP.

2 TR at TJ, no SP (5.5km/3.5 miles). Then, TL, SP Stamfordham. TL at TJ, SP Stamfordham (9.5km/6 miles). Continue to Stamfordham.

3 TR in Stamfordham. Then TR at TJ, SP 10.

4 TR for 200m, SP Ryal. Then TL, SP Reivers.

16.5km (10.5 miles)

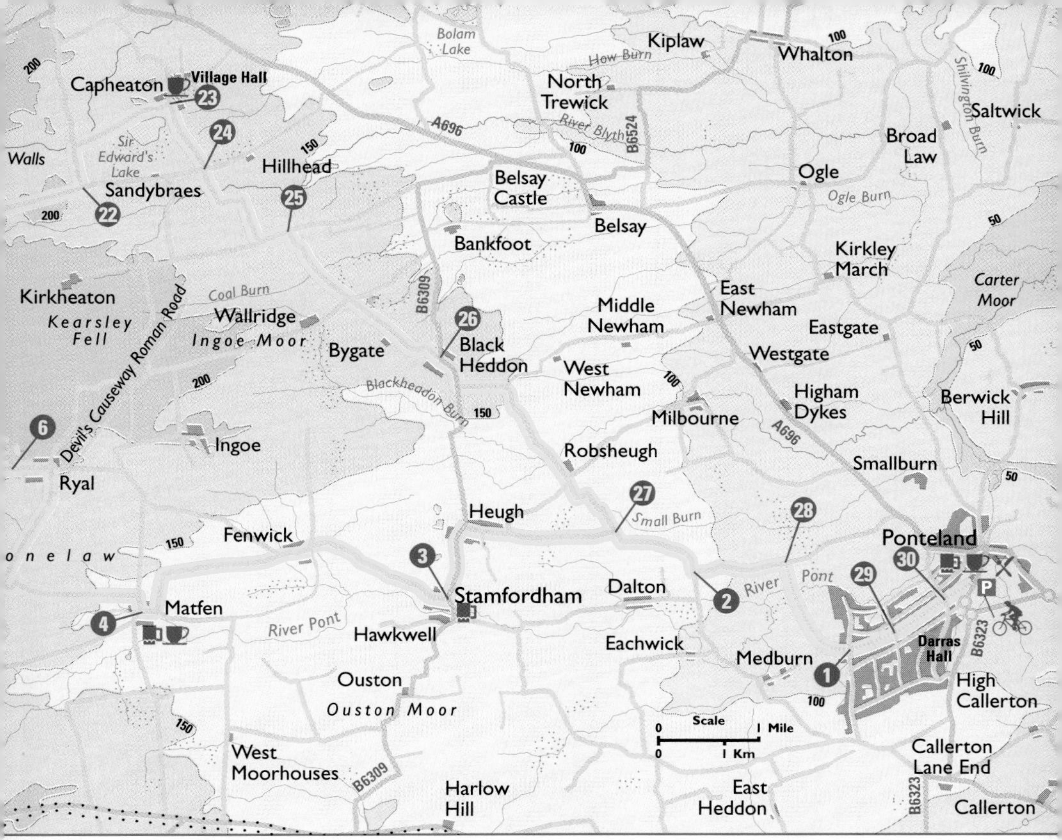

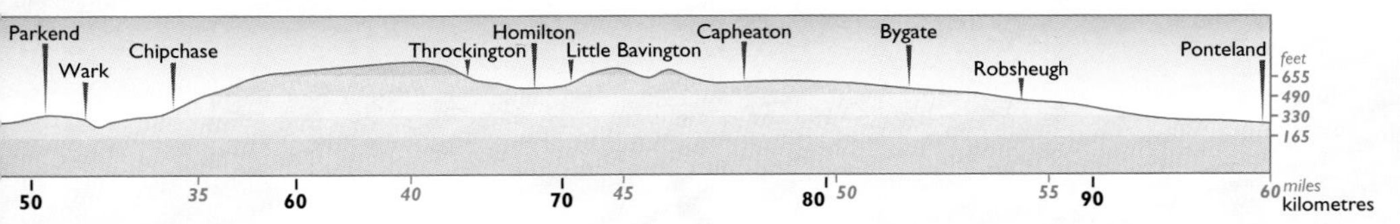

5 TR at TJ, no SP, and continue towards Ryal. TL at XR, SP Reivers.

6 To continue on-road, continue SO (22.5km/14 miles) to direction 7.

To take the off-road option, TR through gate, SP Reivers off-road, and follow well-defined track through West Side Farm to Hallington New House, and back onto tarmac to TJ.

a TR at TJ, SP 10.

b TL through gate onto track, SP Reivers off-road. Continue past Hallington Reservoirs to XR with road.

c TL at XR, no SP. Continue to Colwell.

d TR, SP West Woodburn. Then SO at XR, SP Great Swinburne.

e Take RHF at church (private road on left), through gate onto track for 0.5km (0.3 mile).

St Mungo's Church, Simonburn

Bear left through gate and uphill, ignoring SP bridleway on LHS.

f TL at TJ onto road, no SP. Continue SO down hill, through Gunnerton to TJ.

g TL, SP Barrasford. Continue SO through Barrasford to TJ at Chollerton. Continue route at direction 9, where TR SP Chollerton.

7 SO at XR. Continue to TJ.

28km (17.5 miles)

8 TL at TJ, then immediately SO at XR, SP Chollerford. Continue into Chollerton.

9 SO, SP Chollerford. ***32km (20 miles)***

10 TR at XR, SP Chollerford. Continue into Chollerford, cross bridge over River North Tyne and TR at roundabout, SP Humshaugh. Continue into Humshaugh.

11 TR by Crown Inn, no SP. Follow lane to TJ with main road.

12 TR at TJ, no SP.

13 To visit tearooms, TL, SP Simonburn Tearooms. Otherwise, continue SO into Wark.

14 TR, SP Chipchase Castle. Cross bridge and TR, SP Chipchase Castle.

15 TL, SP Birtley (54km/33.5 miles). TR at next junction, no SP. Continue SO to junction, SP Colwell.

16 TR, SP West Woodburn. Continue to junction with A68.

17 TL onto A68, then TR, SP Kirkwhelpington (use Reivers route track to cross road).

18 TR, SP Throckington. Continue, passing Colt Crag Reservoir.

19 To stay on-road, TL, SP Throckington. Continue through Throckington to TJ with B6342. Continue to direction 20.

To follow the off-road section, SO, SP Little Swinburne. Continue into Little Swinburne. TL at TJ onto track, SP 10. TL at XR onto B6342 and continue SO to rejoin the route at direction 20, where TR, SP Kirkharle.

20 TL, SP Kirkharle. Continue SO, ignoring all SP Reivers.

21 TR, SP Capheaton.

22 TL through gate onto gated road, SP Kirkharle (73km/45.5 miles). Take next TR, through gate, no SP. Continue to Capheaton.

23 TR at TJ, SP Stamfordham.

24 SO at XR, SP Stamfordham. TL at TJ, SP Stamfordham.

25 TR, SP Wallridge. SO at XR, SP Stamfordham.

26 TR at TJ, SP Stamfordham (82.5km/ 51.5 miles). Then TL, SP Ponteland.

27 TL, SP Reivers, for 1.5km (1 mile).

28 TR through gate, SP 10. Continue over road onto bridleway, following SP 10. Continue to junction with road.

29 Bear left at junction, round front of shops and over road, SP Reivers. Retrace route back through red brick estate.

30 SO at XR, staying on track. Then, TR, SP 10, and again TR, SP 10. TL at TJ onto road. TR into Ponteland and return to leisure centre car park to finish the ride.

96.5km (60 miles)

Route 25

NORTHUMBERLAND – A GRANDE RANDONNÉE

Route information

Distance 142.5km (89 miles)

Grade Moderate

Terrain Quiet minor roads. There are two short sections of rough track which can be avoided by using a short section of wide A road.

Time to allow 1–2 days.

Getting there by car From the A1, take A192 into Morpeth town centre. Cross bridge over River Wansbeck, TL at roundabout and continue up main street to corner in front of tower. TL and park by the leisure centre. Leave car park and retrace to roundabout. The Tourist Information Centre (TIC), the starting point, is on the RHS.

Getting there by train There is a railway station in Morpeth. To reach the start of the route, TR down hill out of station. SO over roundabout, past police station to the TIC.

This is a long and beautiful ride covering a large part of Northumberland, taking in Morpeth, Rothbury, Wooler, Alnwick and Warkworth. There are rolling hills, river valleys, open moorland and the coast. The route passes Cragside, the first house in the world to be lit electrically, and dramatic Warkworth Castle. The route may be conveniently broken with an overnight stay in Wooler, where there is a youth hostel, camp site, hotel and bed and breakfast accommodation. Telephone Wooler Tourist Information Centre for details on (01668) 282123.

Places of interest along the route

A Morpeth

The County Town of Northumberland, on the River Wansbeck. Market day is Wednesday and early closing day is Thursday. See route 13 for further details.

B Rothbury

The capital of Coquetdale, this ancient market town is popular with walkers and fishermen. See route 21 for further details.

C Wooler

A small market town in the shadow of the magnificent Cheviot Hills. See route 20 for further details.

D Chillingham Castle, near Alnwick

A medieval fortress with 18th- and 19th-century additions. See route 23 for further details.

E Alnwick

A historical town, connected to the Percy family. Visitors can see the Percy lions, one on top of the Tenantry Tower (on the left as the route enters the town) the other on Lion Bridge to the north of the town. See route 23 for further details.

F Railway marker

Look south along the railway track at the level crossing between Shilbottle and Warkworth.

Warkworth Castle

The marker showing London 300 miles is clearly visible, in a position to be seen from the passing trains.

G Warkworth

A charming village, often busy in the summer. The bridge over the River Coquet on the north side of the village is fortified. **Warkworth Castle** is set high on the peninsula formed by the river and can be seen as the route descends from Shilbottle. The ruins of the 12th- and 15th-century castle are the setting for three scenes from Shakespeare's *Henry IV*. English Heritage property. Open daily, April to September 1000–1800; October 1000–1700; November to March 1000–1600. Telephone (01665) 711423. **Warkworth Hermitage** (also English Heritage) is a curious cut into the rock above the river. Open April to September, Wednesday, Sunday and Bank Holiday Mondays 1100–1700. Telephone as per Warkworth Castle.

N
West Horton
East Horton
Warenton
Lucker
Adderstone
Newhall Hall
West Fleetham
Beadnell
Benthall
Beadnell Bay
Percy Arms Hotel
Greendykes
North Wood
Twizell House
Warenford
Swinhoe
Dismantled railway
Youth Hostel
Wooler
Weetwood Moor
Wandon
Chatton
Newstead
Chathill
Tughall Burn
Tughall
High Newton-by-the-Sea
River Till
Earle
Trickley Wood
Haugh Head
Church Wood
Chillingham
Sandyford Moor
Rosebrough
Ellingham
Broad Wood
Airfield
Middleton Hall
Newtown
Chillingham Castle
Rosebrough Moor
Preston
Brunton
Newton Point
North Middleton
Brands Hill
Hepburn
Low Newton-by-the-Sea
Embleton Bay
South Middleton
East Lilburn
Cateran Hill
Red Burn
Brownieside
Christon Bank
Embleton
Rackside
Roseden Farm
Roseden
Camp Hill
North Charlton
Castle Point
Bewick Moor
Black Burn
Old Bewick
West Ditchburn
Scrog Hill
Dod Hill
Heddon Hill
Wooperton
Harehope Hill
Dunstan Hill
Dunstan
Crag Hill
Shipley Burn
South Charlton
Rock
Craster
New Bewick
Eglingham
Great Wood
Threestoneburn Wood
Stamford
River Breamish
Beanley
Tankerville Arms
Eglingham Burn
Rennington
Cullernose Point
Reaveley Hill
Shipley Wood
Howick
Beanley Plantation
Penny's Petroleum
Reaveley
Powburn
East Bolton
Shipley
Littlehoughton
Howick Haven
Branton
Hartside Hill
Ewe Hill
Longhoughton
Longhoughton Steel
Harlaw Hill
Glanton
Glanton Pyke
West Bolton
Woodhall
Brizlee Hill
Longbank
Boulmer
Cochrane Pike
Bolton
Dunsheugh
Alnwick
Abberwick
Boulmer Haven
Ewe Hill
Great Ryle
Rothill
Hawkhill
River Aln
Prendwick
Lesbury
Whittingham
Battle Bridge
Northfieldhead Hill
Little Ryle
Alnmouth Station
Thrunton
Alnwick Moor or Aydon Forest
Cawledge Burn
Alnham
Bilton
Alnmouth
Thrunton Crag
High Buston
Alnmouth Bay
Yetlington
Callaly
Elilaw
Edlingham
Black Lough
Shilbottle
Northfield

Netherton
Netherton Burnfoot
Lorbottle Hall
Coe Crags
Edlingham Woods
Newton Burn
Southmoor
Eastfield Hall
Railway Marker
Warkworth
Gloster Hill
Coquet Island
High Trewhitt
Lorbottle
Bankhead
Rimside Moor
Swallow Knowe
Newton-on-the-Moor
Cartington
Debdon
B6341
Swarland
Morwick Hall
Amble
Longframlington Common
Lamb Crags
Mere Burn
Snitter
Warton
Debdon Lake
Sun Kitchen
Rothbury
Cragside
Blackburn Lake
A697
Smalldene
Old Swarland
Acklington
B6345
North Togston
Hauxley
Hauxley Haven
Flotterton
Thropton
Coquet
River
Caistron
Little Tosson
Hepple
B6341
Whitton
Cragend
Hope
North End
Swarlanddean
Bondi Carrs
Broomhill
A1068
Hadston Carrs
Great Tosson
Newtown
Longframlington
Mouldshaugh
Felton
East Thirston
B1330
South Broomhill
B6342
B6344
West Row
East Row
Pauperhaugh
Todstead
Bushygap
Swindon
Simonside
Tosson Hill
Chevington Wood
Red Row
Chevington Drift
River Coquet
Howdens
Longdike Burn
The Lee
Forest Burn
Low Hesleyhurst
Westerheugh
West Chevington
Druridge
Whitefield Hill
Selby's Cove
Bywell
Forest Wood
Gunners Box
Forestburn Gate
Spylaw Burn
Chirm
Garrett Lee Wood
Linden East
West Forest
Druridge
Bay
Widdrington
Newbiggin Burn
Harwood
Lough Hill
Wingates
Todburn Moor
West Stobswood
B1337
A1068
Hemmel Hill
Longhorsley
Stobswood
Widdrington Station
Forest
East Stobswood
The Scars
Paxtondean Burn
A697
Fontburn Reservoir
River Font
Rayburn Lake
Earsdon Moor
Cresswell
Snab Point
B6342
Nunnykirk
Beacon Hill
Tritlington
River Lyne
Linton Burn
Ellington
Fenrother
Newpark Wood
Dixon's Wood
The Cockles
Ulgham
Ewesley Burn
Harwood Head
Clayton Fell
Netherwitton
Espley Hall
Bellion
Hebron
B1337
Brock's Burn
Lynemouth
Haydon Letch
A189
Scale
0 1 Mile
0 1 Km
Longwitton
Oldpark Wood
Shelly
Todd Hill
Pigdon
A1
Longhirst
A1068
Woodhorn
Pegswood Moor
Kirkhill
B6342
Wittonstone
Longshaws
River Font
West Benridge
Pegswood
A197
Ashington
Newbiggin-by-the-Sea
Catcherside
Chesters
Newton Underwood
Spital Hill
Hirst
B6343
Bothal
A1068
North Seaton
Blackhalls
Hartburn
Mitford
Morpeth
Castle
Scots' Gap
Cambo
High Angerton
Throphill
B6343
Shadfen
Stakeford
A189
A696
Middleton
Marlish
River Wansbeck
A196
Guide Post
Sheepwash
West Sleekburn

Route description

Start from Morpeth TIC. Head up main street towards clock tower. Follow road to right and up to A1 roundabout.

1 SO at roundabout, SP Alnwick A1/ Coldstream. TL, SP Pigdon/Netherwitton, under bridge (before road joins A1). Continue on this road.

2 TR on fast descent, SP The Lee/Wingates. ***20km (12.5 miles)***

3 SO at XR, SP Pauperhaugh/ Longframlington.

4 TR at TJ and over Pauperhaugh Bridge. ***25km (15.5 miles)***

5 TL at TJ onto B6344, SP Rothbury. Follow this road into Rothbury. Continue through village and into Thropton.

6 TR at Cross Keys pub for steep climb, SP Whittingham/Callaly/Netherton (34.5km/ 21.5 miles). Continue through Callaly into Whittingham.

7 TL at TJ, SP Glanton. Continue into Glanton.

8 TL at TJ, no SP (49km/30.5 miles). Continue into Powburn.

9 TL at TJ onto A697, SP Wooler. To avoid rough tracks, stay on A697 for just over 8km/ 5 miles. TL, SP Middleton, continue into Wooler and rejoin route at direction 26. Otherwise, for off-road continue to direction 10.

10 Cross bridge and immediately TL, no SP.

11 TL at TJ, no SP (53km/33 miles). Continue through Branton.

12 TR, SP No Through Road.

13 Cross the ford via bridge. TR then immediately TL onto track, SP Heddon Hill Cottage.

14 Go through three gates and after third TR onto tarmac.

15 TL through gate (57km/35.5 miles) and continue to Old School House.

16 TR onto track by old school house, SP Bridleway.

17 Continue through gate.

18 SO through gate and descend to TJ (with tarmac) and TR over bridge.

19 TL for Roseden Farm. To continue route, TR at TJ, no SP.

20 TL at TJ, SP Coldstream/Wooler A697.

21 TR, SP Newtown/East Lilburn.

22 TL at TJ, no SP.

23 TR at TJ, over bridge.

24 TR at junction and pass Tower Farm (64km/40 miles). Continue to TJ with A697.

25 TL WITH CARE onto A697, no SP but opposite Glendale Nurseries. Immediately TR onto road (ford ahead). Cross ford and mount rough track. TR at XR with tarmac. Continue into Wooler.

26 TL at TJ into Wooler town centre (71.5km/44.5 miles). Immediately TR into Church Street (steep descent). Then SO at

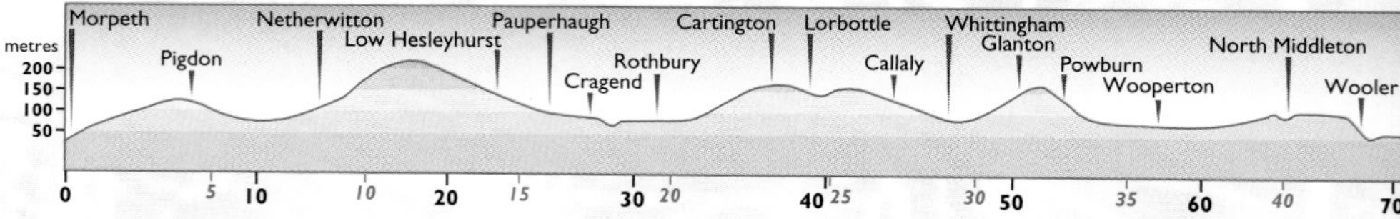

staggered XR, down Weetwood Road (iron bridge here).

27 TR, Chillingham/Alnwick (78.5km/ 49 miles). Pass entrance to Chillingham Castle and continue SO.

28 Continue through Eglingham (91km/ 56.6 miles) into Alnwick to XR (Alnwick Castle gatehouse directly ahead).

29 TR into Narrowgate to town centre. TL at TJ and continue out of town heading north, through Bondgate Arch.

30 TR at roundabout, SP Newcastle/ Morpeth/Berwick A1.

31 TL and under A1 (just after petrol station, 101.5km/63 miles). Immediately TR, SP Shilbottle and Lionheart Enterprise Park.

32 TR at TJ, SP Shilbottle Felton, and continue for steep descent to TJ.

33 TR at TJ, SP Warkworth/Amble (115.5km/72 miles). Follow road through Warkworth, uphill past castle. Continue out of village, past water tower and into Acklington.

34 TR at TJ, SP Felton B6345.

121.5km (75.5 miles)

35 TL on steep bend, SP Eshott/Chevington.

36 TR at TJ, SP Morpeth/Ulgham/B1337 (132km/82.5 miles). Continue through Ulgham and Longhirst to Morpeth.

37 SO at roundabout as enter Morpeth. Then, TR at roundabout, SP Tynemouth/Newcastle/ Alnwick. SO at next roundabout to finish the ride by the TIC. ***142.5km (89 miles)***

Food and drink

There is plenty of choice in Morpeth, Rothbury, Wooler, Alnwick and Warkworth.

Old Bakehouse, Morpeth
In a courtyard on LHS of main street heading north out of town.

Sun Kitchen, Rothbury
Good value, home-cooked meals and snacks.

Penny's Petroleum, Powburn
In the petrol station on the A697, north of the river on the right. A good range of food in pleasant surroundings.

Roseden Farm, Roseden
A well-established farm shop serving excellent home-cooking. Open daily (only full lunches available Sundays).

Percy Arms Hotel, Chatton
Open for lunch and evening bar and restaurant meals.

Tankerville Arms, Eglingham
Open daily for bar meals, 1200–1400 and 1800–2100.

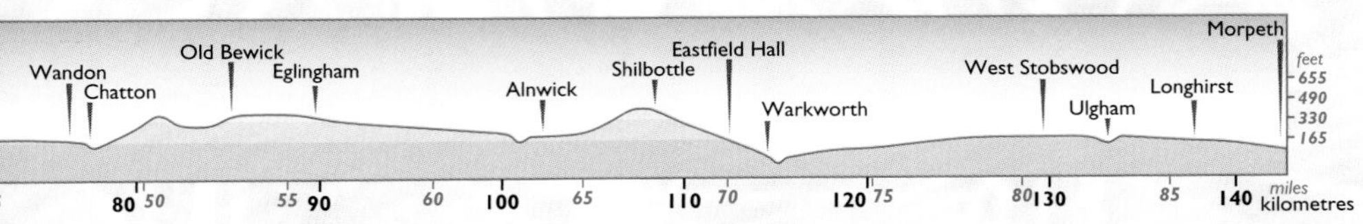

THE CTC

The CTC is Britain's largest national cycling organisation. Founded in 1878, the CTC has over 65,000 members and affiliates throughout the UK, and around 230 local groups. The CTC provides essential services for all leisure cyclists, whether riding on- or off-road, and works to promote cycling and protect cyclists' interests.

Free technical and touring advice

CTC membership makes day-to-day cycling easier. A resident expert cycling engineer answers technical queries about cycle buying, maintenance and equipment. And if you get ambitious about your cycling, the CTC's Touring Department has reams of information about cycling anywhere from Avon to Zimbabwe. Then, when it comes to getting kitted out, the CTC's mail order shop sells a wide variety of clothing and accessories in addition to books, maps and guidebooks, including other titles from HarperCollins Publishers.

CTC Helpdesk – telephone (01483) 417217

CTC members also receive *Cycle Touring and Campaigning* magazine free six times a year. *CT&C* takes pride in its journalistic independence. With reports on cycle trips all over the globe, forensic tests on bikes and equipment, and the most vigorous and effective pro-bike campaigning stance anywhere, *CT&C* is required reading for any cyclist.

CTC membership costs from £15 p.a.

It is not just members who benefit. The CTC works on behalf of all Britain's 22 million cycle owners. Its effective campaigning at national level helped to create the Government's National Cycling Strategy. It is lobbying for lower speed limits on country lanes; campaigning so that you can carry bikes on trains; working with Local Authorities to make towns more cycle-friendly, to ensure that roads are designed to meet cyclists' needs and kept well maintained; making sure that bridleways are kept open; and negotiating cyclists' access to canal towpaths.

Whatever kind of cyclist you are – mountain biker, Sunday potterer, bicycle commuter, or out for the day with your family – cycling is easier and safer with the CTC's knowledge and services in your saddlebag. The CTC is the essential accessory for every cyclist!

For further information contact:
CTC
69 Meadrow
Godalming
Surrey
GU7 3HS

Telephone (01483) 417217
Fax (01483) 426994
e-mail: cycling@ctc.org.uk
Website: http://www.ctc.org.uk